THE PHILOSOPHY OF RHETORIC

THE MARY FLEXNER LECTURES
ON THE HUMANITIES
III

These lectures were delivered at BRYN MAWR COLLEGE,
FEBRUARY and MARCH 1936 on a fund established by
BERNARD FLEXNER in honor of his sister

THE PHILOSOPHY
OF RHETORIC

I. A. RICHARDS

OXFORD UNIVERSITY PRESS
LONDON   OXFORD   NEW YORK

OXFORD UNIVERSITY PRESS
Oxford   London   Glasgow
New York   Toronto   Melbourne   Wellington
Nairobi   Dar es Salaam   Cape Town
Kuala Lumpur   Singapore   Jakarta   Hong Kong   Tokyo
Delhi   Bombay   Calcutta   Madras   Karachi

PREFACE

"PREFACES," wrote Bacon, "and passages, and excusations and other speeches of reference to the person, are great wastes of time ; and though they seem to proceed of modesty, they are bravery." The invitation to give the Mary Flexner Lectures is a greater honour than these outcomes will justify, and the pleasures of my visit to Bryn Mawr and of the association with one of the great names of modern America which the Title of the Lectureship carries are personal matters.

But I may say a word about the form in which these remarks are now offered to the reader's eye — after delivery to an audience's ear. The two modes of utterance rarely agree. None the less I have here kept the written word very close to the spoken, believing that the occasional air is best suited to the tentative provisional spirit in which this subject should at present be treated. May anything that seems extreme in these lectures be thought accidental or be taken as a speaker's device.

I. A. R.

Honolulu, April 7th, 1936

CONTENTS

LECTURE I

INTRODUCTORY

Yet beware of being too material, when there is any impediment or obstruction in men's wills; for preoccupation of mind ever requireth preface of speech; like a fomentation to make the unguent enter.— Francis Bacon, *Of Dispatch.*

LECTURE I

INTRODUCTORY

THESE lectures are an attempt to revive an old subject. I need spend no time, I think, in describing the present state of Rhetoric. Today it is the dreariest and least profitable part of the waste that the unfortunate travel through in Freshman English! So low has Rhetoric sunk that we would do better just to dismiss it to Limbo than to trouble ourselves with it — unless we can find reason for believing that it can become a study that will minister successfully to important needs.

As to the needs, there is little room for doubt about them. Rhetoric, I shall urge, should be a study of misunderstanding and its remedies. We struggle all our days with misunderstandings, and no apology is required for any study which can prevent or remove them. Of course, inevitably *at present*, we have no measure with which to calculate the extent and degree of our hourly losses in communication. One of the aims of these lectures will be to speculate about some of the measures we should require in attempting such estimates. "How much and in how many ways may good communication differ from bad?" That is too big and too complex a question to be answered as it stands, but we can at least try to work towards answering some parts of it; and these explanations would be the revived subject of Rhetoric.

Though we cannot measure our losses in communication we can guess at them. We even have professional guessers: teachers and examiners, whose business is to guess at and diagnose the mistakes other people have made in understanding what they have heard and read and to avoid illustrating these mistakes, if they can, themselves. Another man who is in a good position from which to estimate the current losses in communication is an author looking through a batch of reviews, especially an author who has been writing about some such subject as economics, social or political theory, or criticism. It is not very often that such an author must honestly admit that his reviewers — even when they profess to agree with him — have seen his point. That holds, you may say, only of bad writers who have written clumsily or obscurely. But bad writers are commoner than good and play a larger part in bandying notions about in the world.

The moral from this comes home rather heavily on a Lecturer addressing an audience on such a tangled subject as Rhetoric. It is little use appealing to the hearer as Berkeley did: "I do . . . once for all desire whoever shall think it worth his while to understand . . . that he would not stick in this or that phrase, or manner of expression, but candidly collect my meaning from the whole sum and tenor of my discourse, and laying aside the

words as much as possible, consider the bare notions
themselves. . ."

The trouble is that we *can* only "collect the whole
sum and tenor of the discourse" from the words,
we cannot "lay aside the words"; and as to considering "the bare notions themselves," well, I shall be
considering in a later lecture various notions of a notion and comparing their merits for a study of communication. Berkeley was fond of talking about
these "bare notions," these "naked undisguised
ideas," and about "separating from them all that
dress and encumbrance of words." But an idea or a
notion, when unencumbered and undisguised, is no
easier to get hold of than one of those oiled and naked
thieves who infest the railway carriages of India.
Indeed an idea, or a notion, like the physicist's ulti-
mate particles and rays, is only known by what it does.
Apart from its dress or other signs it is not identi-
fiable. Berkeley himself, of course, has his doubts:
"laying aside the words as much as possible, consider . . ." That "as much as possible" is not very
much; and is not nearly enough for the purposes
for which Berkeley hoped to trust it.

We have instead to consider much more closely
how words work in discourse. But before plunging
into some of the less whelming divisions of this
world-swallowing inquiry, let me glance back for a
few minutes at the traditional treatment of the subject; much might be learnt from it that would help
us. It begins, of course, with Aristotle, and may
perhaps be said to end with Archbishop Whately,

who wrote a treatise on Rhetoric for the *Encyclo-pædia Metropolitana* that Coleridge planned. I may remark, in passing, that Coleridge's own *Essay on Method,* the preface to that Encyclopædia, has itself more bearing on a possible future for Rhetoric than anything I know of in the official literature.

Whately was a prolific writer, but he is most often remembered now perhaps for an epigram. "Woman," he said, "is an irrational animal which pokes the fire from the top." I am not quoting this, here at Bryn Mawr, to prejudice you against the Archbishop : any man, when provoked, might venture such an unwarrantable and imperceptive generalization. But I do hope to prejudice you further against his modes of treating a subject in which he is, according to no less an authority than Jebb, the best modern writer. Whately has another epigram which touches the very heart of our problem, and may be found either comforting or full of wicked possibilities as you please : here it is. "Preachers nobly aim at nothing at all and hit it!" We may well wonder just what the Archbishop meant by that.

What we have to surmise is how Whately, following and summing up the whole history of the subject, can proceed as he did! He says quite truly that "Rhetoric is not one of those branches of study in which we can trace with interest a progressive improvement from age to age" ; he goes on to discuss "whether Rhetoric be worth any diligent cultivation" and to decide, rather half-heartedly, that it is — provided it be taken not as *an* Art of discourse but as *the* Art — that is to say, as a philosophic discipline aiming at a mastery of the fundamental laws of the use of language, not just a set of dodges that will be found to work sometimes. That claim — that Rhetoric must go deep, must take a broad philosophical view of the principles of the Art — is the climax of his Introduction; and yet in the treatise that follows nothing of the sort is attempted, nor is it in any other treatise that I know of. What we are given by Whately instead is a very ably arranged and discussed collection of prudential Rules about the best sorts of things to say in various argumentative situations, the order in which to bring out your propositions and proofs and examples, at what point it will be most effective to disparage your opponent, how to recommend oneself to the audience, and like matters. As to all of which, it is fair to remark, no one ever learned about them from a treatise who did not know about them already; at the best, the treatise may be an occasion for realizing that there is skill to be developed in discourse, but it does not and cannot teach the skill. We can turn on the whole endeavour the words in which the Archbishop derides his arch-enemy Jeremy Bentham: "the proposed plan for the ready exposure of each argument resembles that by which children are deluded, of catching a bird by laying salt on its tail; the existing doubts and difficulties of debate being no greater than, on the proposed system, would be found in determining what Arguments were or were not to be classified" in which places in the system.

Why has this happened? It has happened all through the history of the subject, and I choose Whately because he represents an inherent tendency in its study. When he proceeds from these large-scale questions of the Ordonnance of arguments to the minute particulars of discourse — under the rubric of Style — the same thing happens. Instead of a philosophic inquiry into how words work in discourse, we get the usual postcard's-worth of crude common sense : — be clear, yet don't be dry; be vivacious, use metaphors when they will be understood not otherwise; respect usage; don't be long-winded, on the other hand don't be gaspy; avoid ambiguity; prefer the energetic to the elegant; preserve unity and coherence. . . I need not go over to the other side of the postcard. We all know well enough the maxims that can be extracted by patient readers out of these agglomerations and how helpful we have all found them !

What is wrong with these too familiar attempts to discuss the working of words? How words work is a matter about which every user of language is, of necessity, avidly curious until these trivialities choke the flow of interest. Remembering Whately's recommendation of metaphor, I can put the mistake best perhaps by saying that all they do is to poke the fire from the top. Instead of tackling, in earnest, the problem of how language works at all, they assume that nothing relevant is to be learnt about it ; and that the problem is merely one of disposing the given and unquestioned powers of words to the best advantage. Instead of ventilating by inquiry the sources of the whole action of words, they merely play with generalizations about their effects, generalizations that are uninstructive and unimproving unless we go more deeply and by another route into these grounds. Their conception of the study of language, in brief, is frustratingly distant or macroscopic and yields no return in understanding — either practical or theoretical — unless it is supplemented by an intimate or microscopic inquiry which endeavours to look into the structure of the meanings with which discourse is composed, not merely into the effects of various large-scale disposals of these meanings. In this Rhetoricians may remind us of the Alchemists' efforts to transmute common substances into precious metals, vain efforts because they were not able to take account of the internal structures of the so-called elements.

The comparison that I am using here is one which a modern writer on language can hardly avoid. To account for understanding and misunderstanding, to study the efficiency of language and its conditions, we have to renounce, for a while, the view that words just have their meanings and that what a discourse does is to be explained as a composition of these meanings — as a wall can be represented as a composition of its bricks. We have to shift the focus of our analysis and attempt a deeper and more minute grasp and try to take account of the

structures of the smallest discussable units of meaning and the ways in which these vary as they are put
with other units.   Bricks, for all practical purposes,
hardly mind what other things they are put with.
Meanings mind intensely — more indeed than any
other sorts of things.   It is the peculiarity of meanings that they do so mind their company; that is in
part what we mean by calling them meanings!   In
themselves they are nothing — figments, abstractions,
unreal things that we invent, if you like — but we
invent them for a purpose.   They help us to avoid
taking account of the peculiar way in which any
part of a discourse, in the last resort, does what it
does only because the other parts of the surround-
ing, uttered or unuttered discourse and its conditions are what they are.   "In the last resort" — the
last resort here is mercifully a long way off and very
deep down.   Short of it we are aware of certain
stabilities which hide from us this universal rela-
tivity or, better, interdependence of meanings.
Some words and sentences still more, do seem to
mean what they mean absolutely and uncondition-
ally.   This is because the conditions governing their
meanings are so constant that we can disregard them.
So the weight of a cubic centimeter of water seems a
fixed and absolute thing because of the constancy of
its governing conditions.   In weighing out a pound
of tea we can forget about the mass of the earth.
And with words which have constant conditions the
common sense view that they have fixed proper
meanings, which should be learned and observed, is

justified.   But these words are fewer than we suppose.   Most words, as they pass from context to
context, change their meanings ; and in many different ways.   It is their duty and their service to us
to do so.   Ordinary discourse would suffer anchy-
losis if they did not, and so far we have no ground
for complaint.   We are extraordinarily skilful in
some fields with these shifts of sense — especially
when they are of the kind we recognize officially as
metaphor.   But our skill fails; it is patchy and
fluctuant ; and, when it fails, misunderstanding of
others and of ourselves comes in.

A chief cause of misunderstanding, I shall argue
later, is the Proper Meaning Superstition.   That is,
the common belief — encouraged officially by what
lingers on in the school manuals as Rhetoric — that
a word has a meaning of its own (ideally, only one)
independent of and controlling its use and the
purpose for which it should be uttered.   This
superstition is a recognition of a certain kind of
stability in the meanings of certain words.   It is
only a superstition when it forgets (as it commonly
does) that the stability of the meaning of a word
comes from the constancy of the contexts that give
it its meaning.   Stability in a word's meaning is not
something to be assumed, but always something to
be explained.   And as we try out explanations, we
discover, of course, that — as there are many sorts
of constant contexts — there are many sorts of stabilities.   The stability of the meaning of a word like
knife, say, is different from the stability of a word like

mass in its technical use, and then again both differ from the stabilities of such words, say, as *event, ingression, endurance, recurrence,* or *object,* in the paragraphs of a very distinguished predecessor in this Lectureship.   It will have been noticed perhaps that the way I propose to treat meanings has its analogues with Mr. Whitehead's treatment of things.   But indeed no one to whom Berkeley has mattered will be very confident as to which is which.

I have been suggesting—with my talk of macroscopic and microscopic inquiries—that the theory of language may have something to learn, not much but a little, from the ways in which the physicist envisages stabilities.   But much closer analogies are possible with some of the patterns of Biology.   The theory of interpretation is obviously a branch of biology—a branch that has not grown very far or very healthily yet.   To remember this may help us to avoid some traditional mistakes—among them the use of bad analogies which tie us up if we take them too seriously.   Some of these are notorious; for example, the opposition between form and content, and the almost equivalent opposition between matter and form.   These are wretchedly inconvenient metaphors.   So is that other which makes language a dress which thought puts on.   We shall do better to think of a meaning as though it were a plant that has grown—not a can that has been filled or a lump of clay that has been moulded.   These are obvious inadequacies; but, as the history of criticism shows, they have not been avoided, and the

perennial efforts of the reflective to amend or sur-
pass them — Croce is the extreme modern example
— hardly help.

More insidious and more devastating are the over-
simple mechanical analogies which have been
brought in under the heading of Associationism in
the hope of explaining how language works. And
thought as well. The two problems are close together and similar and neither can be discussed profitably apart from the other. But, unless we drastically remake their definitions, and thereby dodge the
main problems, Language and Thought are not —
need I say? — one and the same. I suppose I must,
since the Behaviorists have so loudly averred that
Thought is sub-vocal talking. That however is a
doctrine I prefer, in these lectures, to attack by implication. To discuss it explicitly would take time that
can, I think, be spent more fruitfully. I will only
say that I hold that any doctrine identifying Thought
with *muscular* movement is a self-refutation of the
observationalism that prompts it — heroic and fatal.
And that an identification of Thought with an activity of the nervous system is to me an acceptable hy-
pothesis, but too large to have interesting applications. It may be left until more is known about
both; when possibly it may be developed to a point
at which it might become useful. At present it is
still Thought which is most accessible to study and
accessible largely through Language. We can all de-
tect a difference in our own minds between thinking
of a dog and thinking of a cat. But no neurologist

can. Even when no cats or dogs are about and we are doing nothing about them except thinking of them, the difference is plainly perceptible. We can also say 'dog' and think 'cat.'

I must, though, discuss the doctrine of associations briefly, because when we ask ourselves about how words mean, some theory about trains of associated ideas or accompanying images is certain to occur to us as an answer. And until we see how little distance these theories take us they are frustrating. We all know the outline of these theories: we learn what the word 'cat' means by seeing a cat at the same time that we hear the word 'cat' and thus a link is formed between the sight and the sound. Next time we hear the word 'cat' an image of a cat (a visual image, let us say) arises in the mind, and that is how the word 'cat' means a cat. The obvious objections that come from the differences between cats; from the fact that images of a grey persian asleep and of a tabby stalking are very different, and from some people saying they never have any imagery, must then be taken account of, and the theory grows very complex. Usually, images get relegated to a background and become mere supports to something hard to be precise about —an idea of a cat—which is supposed then to be associated with the word 'cat' much as the image originally was supposed to be associated with it.

This classical theory of meaning has been under heavy fire from many sides for more than a century —from positions as different as those of Coleridge, of Bradley, of Pavlov and of the *gestalt* psychologists. In response it has elaborated itself, calling in the aid of the conditioned-reflex and submitting to the influence of Freud. I do not say that it is incapable, when amended, of supplying us with a workable theory of meaning — in fact, in the next lecture I shall sketch an outline theory of how words mean which has associationism among its obvious ancestors. And here, in saying that simple associationism does not go far enough and is an impediment unless we see this, I am merely reminding you that a clustering of associated images and ideas about a word in the mind does not answer our question: "How does a word mean?" It only hands it on to them, and the question becomes: "How does an idea (or an image) mean what it does?" To answer that we have to go outside the mind and inquire into its connections with what are not mental occurrences. Or (if you prefer, instead, to extend the sense of the word 'mind') we have to inquire into connections between events which were left out by the traditional associationism. And in leaving them out they left out the problem.

For our purposes here the important points are two. First, that ordinary, current, undeveloped associationism is ruined by the crude inapposite physical metaphor of impressions stamped on the mind (the image of the cat stamped by the cat), impressions then linked and combined in clusters like atoms in molecules. That metaphor gives us no useful account either of perception or of reflection, and we shall not be able to think into or think out any of the interesting problems of Rhetoric unless we improve it.

Secondly the appeal to *imagery* as constituting the meaning of an utterance has, in fact, frustrated a large part of the great efforts that have been made by very able people ever since the 17th Century to put Rhetoric back into the important place it deserves among our studies. Let me give you an example. Here is Lord Kames — who, as a Judge of the Court of Session in Scotland, was not without a reputation for shrewdness — being, I believe, really remarkably silly.

In *Henry V* (Act IV, scene I) Williams in a fume says this of what "a poor and private displeasure can do against a monarch": "You may as well go about to turn the sun to ice with fanning in his face with a peacock's feather." Lord Kames comments, "The peacock's feather, not to mention the beauty of the object, completes the image : an accurate image cannot be formed of that fanciful operation without conceiving a particular feather ; and one is at a loss when this is neglected in the description." (*Elements of Criticism*, p. 372.)

That shows, I think, what the imagery obsession can do to a reader. Who in the world, apart from a theory, would be "at a loss" unless the sort of feather we are to fan the sun's face with is specified? If we cared to be sillier than our author, we could pursue him on his theory, by asking whether it is to be a long or a short feather or whether the sun is at its height or setting? The whole theory that the point of Shakespeare's specification is to "complete the image," in Kames' sense, is utterly mistaken and misleading. What *peacock* does, in the context there, is obviously to bring in considerations that heighten the idleness, the vanity, in Williams' eyes, of "poor and private displeasures against a monarch." A peacock's feather is something one might flatter oneself with. Henry has said that if the King lets himself be ransomed he will never trust his word after. And Williams is saying, "You'll never trust his word after! What's that! Plume yourself upon it as much as you like, but what will that do to the king!"

Lord Kames in 1761, blandly enjoying the beauty and completeness of the lively and distinct and accurate image of the feather he has produced for himself, and thereby missing, it seems, the whole tenor of the passage, is a spectacle worth some attention.

I shall be returning to Lord Kames, in a later lecture, when I discuss metaphor. His theories about trains of ideas and images are typical 18th Century Associationism — the Associationism of which David Hartley is the great prophet — and the applications of these theories in the detail of Rhetoric are their own refutation. We have to go beyond these theories, but however mistaken they may be, or however absurd their outcome may sometimes seem, we must not forget that they are beginnings, first steps in a great and novel venture, the attempt to explain in detail how language works and with it to improve communication. As such, these attempts merit the most discerning and the most sympathetic eye that we can turn upon them. Indeed, it is impossible to read Hartley, for example, without deep sympathy if we realize what a task it was that he was attempting. Not only when he writes, in his conclusion, in words which speak the thoughts of every candid inquirer: "This is by no means a full or satisfactory Account of the Ideas which adhere to words by Association. For the Author perceives himself to be still a mere novice in these speculations; and it is difficult to explain Words to the Bottom by Words; perhaps impossible." (On Man, 277.) But still more when he says: "All that has been delivered by the Ancients and Moderns, concerning the power of Habit, Custom, Example, Education, Authority, Party-prejudice, the Manner of learning the manual and liberal Arts, Etc., goes upon this Doctrine as its foundation, and may be considered as the detail of it, in various circumstances. I hope here to begin with the simplest case, and shall proceed to more and more complex ones continually, till I have exhausted what has occurred to me on this Subject." (On Man, p. 67.)

The man who wrote that was not 'poking the fire from the top.' His way of ventilating the subject may not have been perfectly advised, but he saw what needed doing and it is no wonder that Coleridge for a while admired Hartley beyond all other men. For upon the formation and transformations of meanings — which we must study with and through words

— all that Hartley mentions, and much more, goes as its foundation. For it is no exaggeration to say that the fabrics of all our various worlds are the fabrics of our meanings. I began, you recall, with Berkeley, with — to use Mr. Yeats' noble lines —

God appointed Berkeley who proved all things a dream,
That this preposterous pragmatical pig of a world, its
    farrow that so solid seem,
Must vanish on the instant did the mind but change its
    theme.

Whatever we may be studying we do so only through the growth of our meanings. To realize this turns some parts of this attempted direct study of the modes of growth and interaction between meanings, which might otherwise seem a niggling philosophic juggle with distinctions, into a business of great practical importance. For this study is theoretical only that it may become practical. Here is the paragraph in which Hobbes condenses what he had learnt from his master, Bacon :

"The end or scope of philosophy is, that we may make use to our benefit of effects formerly seen, or that, by the application of bodies to one another, we may produce the like effects of those we conceive in our mind, as far forth as matter, strength and industry, will permit, for the commodity of human life. For the inward glory and triumph of mind that a man may have for the mastery of some difficult and doubtful matter, or for the discovery of some hidden truth, is not worth so much pains as the study of Philosophy requires ; nor need any man care much to teach another what he knows himself, if he think that will be the only benefit of his labour. The end of knowledge

is power ; and the use of theorems (which, among
geometricians, serve for the finding out of properties)
is for the construction of problems ; and, lastly, the
scope of all speculation is the performance of some
action, or thing to be done."

I shall go on then, in the next Lecture, by the use
of theorems to the construction of problems, without
further insisting that these problems are those upon
which, wittingly and unwittingly, we spend our
whole waking life.

LECTURE II

THE AIMS OF DISCOURSE AND TYPES OF CONTEXT

I repeat, however, that there is a prime part of education, an element of the basis itself, in regard to which I shall probably remain within the bounds of safety in declaring that no explicit, no separate, no adequate plea will be likely to have ranged itself under any one of your customary heads of commemoration.— Henry James, A Commemoration Address at Bryn Mawr on *The Question of our Speech.*

LECTURE II

THE AIMS OF DISCOURSE AND TYPES OF CONTEXT

IN MY introductory lecture I urged that there is room for a persistent, systematic, detailed inquiry into how words work that will take the place of the discredited subject which goes by the name of Rhetoric.   I went on to argue that this inquiry must be philosophic, or — if you hesitate with that word, I do myself — that it must take charge of the criticism of its own assumptions and not accept them, more than it can help, ready-made from other studies. How words mean, is not a question to which we can safely accept an answer either as an inheritance from common sense, that curious growth, or as something vouched for by another science, by psychology, say — since other sciences use words themselves and not least delusively when they address themselves to these questions.   The result is that a revived Rhetoric, or study of verbal understanding and misunderstanding, must itself undertake its own inquiry into the modes of meaning — not only, as with the old Rhetoric, on a macroscopic scale, discussing the effects of different disposals of large parts of a discourse — but also on a microscopic scale by using theorems about the structure of the fundamental conjectural units of meaning and the conditions through which they, and their interconnections, arise.

In the old Rhetoric, of course, there is much that a new Rhetoric finds useful — and much besides which may be advantageous until man changes his nature, debates and disputes, incites, tricks, bullies and cajoles his fellows less. Aristotle's notes on the forensic treatment of evidence elicited under torture are unhappily not without their utility still in some very up-to-date parts of the world.

Among the general themes of the old Rhetoric there is one which is especially pertinent to our inquiry. The old Rhetoric was an offspring of dispute; it developed as the rationale of pleadings and persuadings; it was the theory of the battle of words and has always been itself dominated by the combative impulse. Perhaps what it has most to teach us is the narrowing and blinding influence of that preoccupation, that debaters' interest.

Persuasion is only one among the aims of discourse. It poaches on the others — especially on that of *exposition*, which is concerned to state a view, not to persuade people to agree or to do anything more than examine it. The review and correspondence columns of the learned and scientific journals are the places in which to watch this poaching at its liveliest. It is no bad preparation for any attempt at exposition— above all of such debatable and contentious matters as those to which I am soon to turn — to realize how easily the combative impulse can put us in mental blinkers and make us take an-

other man's words in the ways in which we can down
him with least trouble.

I can point this moral — call it defensive if you will
— with a small specimen from one of the many little
books which in the Nineteenth Century attempted
a reform of Rhetoric.   It is from Benjamin Hum-
phrey Smart's *Practical Logic,* a little book written
for and used for a few decades in the best young
ladies' seminaries through the middle of the Nineteenth Century and now as dead as any book well
can be.   Smart is discussing the conduct of exposition.   He has listed a number of faults commonly
committed and comes to the

TENTH FAULT TO BE AVOIDED, namely: *Forgetting the Proposition.*

"Of this error," he writes, "the following instance
may suffice :

> 'Anger has been called a short madness ; and people
> of the weakest understanding are the most subject to it.
> It is remarkable that when a disputant is in the wrong,
> he tries to make up in violence what he wants in
> argument.   This arises from his pride.   He will not
> own his error, and because he is determined not to be
> convicted of it, he falls into a passion.'

Here, (Smart comments) instead of going on to show
why Anger has been called a short madness, the
writer wanders into reflections which have no necessary connection with the particular proposition.
He should have reasoned thus :

> 'Anger has been called a short madness.   To be con-
> vinced that the appellation is just, let us look to the

effects of anger. It disturbs a man's judgment, so that he inflicts an injury on his dearest friend, who, the next moment, he loads with caresses. It makes him run headlong into dangers, which, if his mind were clear, he would be the first to see and avoid. It is true that anger does not always disturb the mind to this degree, but that it always disturbs the mind in a degree proportional to its violence, is certain ; and therefore it may be justly characterised as a madness.' "

What necessary connection with the proposition, may we ask, has this sketch of some scenes from an early Victorian Novel? And whence comes this certainty that anger *always* disturbs the mind in a degree proportional to its violence? However, it is better perhaps to take its lesson to heart and remember that anger is not the only warping passion. Risibility and tedium, too, I think Smart would have said, can disturb the judgment.

Warned now of the dangers both of forgetting the proposition and of the 'short madness' that the combative and other passions induce, let me sketch, to use Hobbes' words, a theorem about meanings which may be useful in constructing the most general problems of a new Rhetoric.

I had better put in another warning, though, here. What follows is unavoidably abstract and general in the extreme. It may therefore rather illustrate the difficulties of communicating with such highly abstract language than achieve as much communication as we would wish. If so the fault will not lie, I hope and believe, either in my stupidity or in our joint stupidity. It will lie in the abstractness of the language. It has to be abstract here. What it is trying to say cannot, I think, be put safely in more concrete terms, for it is not talking about this or that mode of meaning but about all meanings. And I cannot here start with illustrations, because all things equally illustrate what I am saying; and how they are to be taken is just the problem. But, after this bout of abstractions, the applications I shall be making in the later Lectures will, I believe, clear up this dark patch. In brief, how we use this theorem best shows us what the theorem is.

If, then, you seem in the next half hour at times merely to be hearing words as sounds that come and go, I must beg your indulgence, or buy it with the promise that we *shall* come out again to practical problems in the everyday conduct of words. Meanwhile this very difficulty is an illustration of a chief practical problem.

What I am now going to try to say is something which, if it is right, we all in a sense know extremely well already.   "It is not sufficiently considered," said Dr. Johnson, "that men more frequently require to be reminded than informed."   I shall be trying to remind you of something so simple that it is hard to think of.   Something as simple as possible, and, to quote Hobbes again, "clear and perspicuous to all men — save only to those who studying the hard writings of the metaphysicians, which they believe to be some egregious learning, think they understand not when they do."   And it may be comforting to recall that Lotze began a course of lectures

on an allied subject by saying that "The simplest
of the conceptions here employed, that of a thing
and that of its being, however lucid they appear
at first, on closer consideration grow always more
and more obscure." For 'always' I would say
'for a time.' We return to lucidity. But now to
work.

I have two sets of problems in view : one set I have
just been talking about — the division of the various
aims of discourse, the purposes for which we speak
or write ; in brief, the functions of language. The
other set of problems goes deeper, and, if we can set
it rightly, the problems about the language functions are best approached from it. I can indicate
these deeper problems in many ways : What is the
connection between the mind and the world by
which events in the mind mean other events in the
world ? Or "How does a thought come to be 'of'
whatever it is that it is a thought of ?" or "What is
the relation between a thing and its name ?" The
last indication may not seem to carry as far as the
others ; but they are all the same problem and I put
the 'name'-formulation in because an over-simple
view of naming, or rather a treatment of words in
general as though they were names (usually of ideas)
has been a main defect in the traditional study.
These are, you will see, really deep problems. As
such we shall not expect any answers which will be
satisfactory. We must be content if the answers we
get are to some degree useful — useful among other
things in improving themselves.

I can start the theorem safely by remarking that we are things peculiarly responsive to other things. To develop this we have to consider the peculiarities of our responsiveness. We are responsive in all sorts of ways. Some of these ways are relatively simple, if cut short enough ; as when we jump at a loud noise or respond to changes of temperature. But even here, if we compare ourselves to thermometers, we see that our responses are of a different order of complexity. A thermometer responds, the length of its thread of mercury varies with the temperature, but only with the present temperature — unless the thermometer is a bad one. What has happened to it in the past, what temperatures it formerly recorded, and the order in which it recorded them, all that has no bearing upon and does not interfere with its present response to changes of temperature. We can imagine, though, a thermometer that, whenever the temperature went up and down like this, M, did something that could only be explained by bringing in other things that happened to it in the past when the temperature went up and down so, M. And correspondingly did something else whenever the temperature went down and up, W. Such an imaginary thermometer would be on the way to showing characteristics of the behavior of living systems, of the systems which, we say, have a mind.

Now consider our own minds' simplest operations. Do we ever respond to a stimulus in a way which is not influenced by the other things that happened to us when more or less similar stimuli struck us in the past? Probably never. A new kind of stimulus might perhaps give rise to a new kind of sensation, a new kind of pain, say. But even so we should probably recognize it as a pain of some sort. Effects from more or less similar happenings in the past would come in to give our response its character and this as far as it went would be meaning. Meaning of a lowly kind, no doubt, the kind of meaning that the least developed animals live by. It is important — and that is why I have started so far back with these elementaries — to realize how far back into the past all our meanings go, how they grow out of one another much as an organism grows, and how inseparable they are from one another.

I can make the same point by denying that we have any sensations. That sounds drastic but is almost certainly true if rightly understood. A sensation would be something that just was *so*, on its own, a datum; as such we have none. Instead we have perceptions, responses whose character comes to them from the past as well as the present occasion. A perception is never just of an *it;* perception takes whatever it perceives as a thing of a certain sort. All thinking from the lowest to the highest — whatever else it may be — is sorting.

That is an important part of the theorem because it removes, if it is accepted, one of the worst troubles which have distorted traditional accounts of the meanings of words — the troubles that gave rise to the Nominalist, Realist, Conceptual controversies

best known to us through the great British philosophical battle of the Eighteenth Century about
whether we have and how we come by abstract ideas
and what they are. This theorem alleges that
meanings, from the very beginning, have a primordial generality and abstractness ; and it follows William James in saying that the lowliest organism — a
polyp or an amoeba — if it learns at all from its past,
if it exclaims in its acts, "Hallo! Thingembob
again!" thereby shows itself to be a conceptual
thinker. It is behaving or thinking with a concept
— not, of course, *of* one. Its act is abstractive and
general ; disregards in some respects the former situations and so is abstractive, and applies in some
respects not to one single thing but to any of a sort
and so is general.

The theorem settles the Eighteenth Century problem by standing it on its head. That problem was,
How do we manage, from this particular concrete
thing and that particular concrete thing and the
other particular concrete thing, to arrive at the general abstract anything? The theorem holds that we
begin with the general abstract anything, split it, as
the world makes us, into sorts and then arrive at
concrete particulars by the overlapping or common
membership of these sorts. This bit of paper here
now in my hand is a concrete particular to us so far
as we think of it as paperish, hereish, nowish and
in my hand ; it is the more concrete as we take it as
of more sorts, and the more specific as the sorts are
narrower and more exclusive.

The next step in the theorem takes us on to words and their meanings. If we sum up thus far by saying that meaning is *delegated efficacy,* that description applies above all to the meaning of words, whose virtue is to be substitutes exerting the powers of what is not there. They do this as other signs do it, though in more complex fashions, through their contexts.

I must explain now the rather special and technical sense I am giving to this word 'context.' This is the pivotal point of the whole theorem. The word has a familiar sense in 'a literary context,' as the other words before and after a given word which determine how it is to be interpreted. This is easily extended to cover the rest of the book. I recall the painful shock I suffered when I first came across, in a book by Dr. Bosanquet, what he called the Golden Rule of Scholarship, "Never to quote or comment on anything in a book which you have not read from cover to cover." As with other Golden Rules a strange peace would fall upon the world if that were observed. I cannot honestly say I either practice the Rule or recommend it. There is a middle way wiser for the Children of this World. However, as I neither am nor hope to be a scholar, I have no occasion to practise it.

The familiar sense of 'context' can be extended further to include the circumstances under which anything was written or said ; wider still to include, for a word in Shakespeare, say, the other known uses of the word about that time, wider still finally to include anything whatever about the period, or about anything else which is relevant to our interpretation of it. The technical use I am going to make of this term 'context' is none of these — though it has something in common with them as having to do with the governing conditions of an interpretation. We can get to it best, perhaps, by considering those recurrences in nature which statements of causal laws are about.

Put very simply, a causal law may be taken as saying that, under certain conditions, of two events if one happens the other does. We usually call the first the cause and the second the effect, but the two may happen together, as when I clap my hands and both palms tingle. If we are talking about final causes we reverse them, and the lecture you are going to hear was the cause of your coming hither. There is a good deal of arbitrariness at several points here which comes from the different purposes for which we need causal laws. We decide, to suit these purposes, how we shall divide up events; we make the existence of the earth one event and the tick of a clock another, and so on. And we distribute the titles of 'cause' and 'effect' as we please. Thus we do not please to say that night causes day or day night. We prefer to say that given the conditions the rotation of the earth is the cause of their succession. We are especially arbitrary in picking out the cause from among the whole group, or context, of conditions — of prior and subsequent events which hang together. Thus the coroner decides that the cause of a man's death was the act of a murderer and not the man's meeting with the murderer, or the stopping of his heart, or the fact that he was not wearing a bullet-proof waistcoat. That is because the coroner is interested in certain kinds of causal laws but not in others. So here, in sketching this causal theorem of meaning, I am interested only in certain kinds of law and am not necessarily saying anything about others.

Now for the sense of 'context.' Most generally it is a name for a whole cluster of events that recur together — including the required conditions as well as whatever we may pick out as cause or effect. But the modes of causal recurrence on which meaning depends are peculiar through that delegated efficacy I have been talking about. In these contexts one item — typically a word — takes over the duties of parts which can then be omitted from the recurrence. There is thus an abridgement of the context only shown in the behavior of living things, and most extensively and drastically shown by man. When this abridgement happens, what the sign or word — the item with these delegated powers — means is the missing parts of the context.

If we ask how this abridgement happens, how a sign comes to stand for an absent cause and conditions, we come up against the limits of knowledge at once. No one knows. Physiological speculation has made very little progress towards explaining *that*, though enormous strides have been made this century in analysing the complexities of the conditioned reflex. The shift, the handing over, is left still as inexplicable. Probably this 'learning problem' goes down as deep as the nature of life itself. We can suppose, if we like, that some sorts of residual effects are left behind from former occurrences which later co-operate with the sign in determining the response. To do so is to use a metaphor drawn from the gross behavior, taken macroscopically, of systems that are not living—printed things, gramaphone records and such. We can be fairly ingenious with these metaphors, invent neural archives storing up impressions, or neural telephone exchanges with fantastic properties. But how the archives get consulted or how in the telephone system A gets on to the B it needs, instead of to the whole alphabet at once in a jumble, remain utterly mysterious matters.

Fortunately linguistics and the theory of meaning need not wait until this is remedied. They can probably go much further than we have yet imagined without any answer to this question. It is enough for our purposes to say that what a word means is the missing parts of the contexts from which it draws its delegated efficacy.

At this point I must remind you of what I said a few minutes ago about the primordial generality and abstractness of meaning and about how, when we mean the simplest-seeming concrete object, its concreteness comes to it from the way in which we are bringing it simultaneously into a number of sorts. The sorts grow together in it to form that meaning. Theory here, as so often, can merely exploit the etymological hint given in the word 'concrete.'

If we forget this and suppose that we start with discrete impressions of particulars ('fixities and definites' as Coleridge called them) and then build these up into congeries, the theorem I am recommending collapses at once into contradictions and absurdities. That was the fault of the old Hartleian Associationism I complained of last time. It did not go back far enough, it took particular impressions as its initial terms. But the initial terms for this theorem are not impressions; they are sortings, recognitions, laws of response, recurrences of like behaviors.

A particular impression is already a product of concrescence. Behind, or in it, there has been a coming together of *sortings*. When we take a number of particular impressions — of a number of different white things, say — and abstract from them an idea of whiteness, we are explicitly reversing a process which has already been implicitly at work in our perception of them as all white. Our risk is to confuse the abstractness we thus arrive at intellectually with the primordial abstractness out of which these impressions have already grown — before ever any conscious explicit reflection took place.

Things, in brief, are instances of laws. As Bradley said, association marries only universals, and out of these laws, these recurrent likenessess of behavior, in our minds and in the world — not out of revived duplicates of individual past impressions — the fabric of our meanings, which is the world, is composed.

So much for the theorem. What are the problems we must use it to construct?

Since the whole business of Rhetoric comes down to comparisons between the meanings of words, the first problem, I think, should be this. How, if the meaning of a word is, in this sense, the missing parts of its contexts, how then should we compare the meanings of two words? There is opportunity for a grand misunderstanding here. It is not proposed that we should try to make these comparisons by a process of discovering, detailing, and then comparing these missing parts. We could not do it and, if we could, it would be waste of time. The theorem does not pretend to give us quite new ways of distinguishing between meanings. It only bars out certain practices and assumptions which are common and misleading.

The office of the theorem is much more negative than positive ; but is not the less useful for that. It will not perhaps tell us how to do much that we cannot do without it already ; but it will prevent us from doing stupid things which we are fond of doing. So a theory of evolution at least makes it more difficult to believe that The Dog Fritz in the German account really did the children's sums for them, or reminded them to salute their 'dear German flag.' So even an elementary physics puts in its place among superstitions Mr. Gladstone's firm belief that snow has "a peculiar power of penetrating leather," a power not possessed by water ! For lack of that knowledge of physics in Mr. Gladstone, Lord

Rayleigh found it quite impossible to persuade him it was not so.

The context theorem of meaning would prevent our making hundreds of baseless and disabling assumptions that we commonly make about meanings, over-simplifications that create false problems interfering with closer comparisons — and that is its main service.   In this, it belongs with a number of other theorems which may be called policeman doctrines — because they are designed on the model of an ideal police-force, not to make any of us do anything but to prevent other people from interfering unduly with our lawful activities.   The organization of impulses doctrine of values for literary criticism is in the same position.   These policeman doctrines keep assumptions that are out of place from frustrating and misleading sagacity.   I shall be illustrating the restraint of these bullying assumptions in most parts of Rhetoric later.   We had one simple instance with Lord Kames' peacock's feather, last time, where what was discouraged was a naïve view of imagery as the stuff of meaning.

We shall have others in discussing the claims of usage next week.   Preëminently what the theorem would discourage, is our habit of behaving as though, if a passage means one thing it cannot at the same time mean another and an incompatible thing. Freud taught us that a dream may mean a dozen different things ; he has persuaded us that some symbols are, as he says, 'over-determined' and mean many different selections from among their causes.

This theorem goes further, and regards all discourse — outside the technicalities of science — as over-determined, as having multiplicity of meaning. It can illustrate this view from almost any of the great controversies. And it offers us — by restraining the One and Only One True Meaning Superstition — a better hope, I believe, of profiting from the controversies. A controversy is normally an exploitation of a systematic set of misunderstandings for war-like purposes. This theorem suggests that the swords of dispute might be turned into plough shares ; and a way found by which we may (to revert to Hobbes) "make use to our benefit of effects formerly seen — for the commodity of human life."

The next problem concerns what happens when we put words together in sentences. At least that is a common way of stating it. The theorem recommends us rather to turn the problem round and ask what happens when, out of the integral utterance which is the sentence, we try to isolate the discrete meanings of the words of which it is composed. That problem, the analysis of sentences and the interaction between words in the sentence, is my subject for next week. It is there that the most deep-rooted, systematic and persistent misunderstandings arise.

A third set of problems concerns rivalries between different types of context which supply the meaning for a single utterance. These start with the plain equivoque — as when the word 'reason' may mean either a cause or an argument. I am simplifying

this here to make it a type of a really simple ambiguity. Actually in most occurrences it would be
much more complex and not so easily cleared up,
as the shifting meanings of 'cause' and 'argument'
themselves show. The context theorem of meaning will make us expect ambiguity to the widest extent and of the subtlest kinds nearly everywhere,
and of course we find it. But where the old Rhetoric
treated ambiguity as a fault in language, and hoped
to confine or eliminate it, the new Rhetoric sees it as
an inevitable consequence of the powers of language
and as the indispensable means of most of our most
important utterances — especially in Poetry and Religion.   And that too I shall be illustrating later.

Of course ambiguities are a nuisance in exposition
as, in spite of my efforts, you have certainly been
feeling. But neutral exposition is a very special
limited use of language, comparatively a late development to which we have not (outside some
parts of the sciences) yet adapted it. This brings
me to those large-scale rivalries between contexts
which shift the very aims of discourse. When the
passions — the combative passion and others — inter-
vene, either in the formation of an utterance or in
its interpretation, we have examples of context
action just as much as when the word 'paper,' say,
takes its meaning from its contexts. The extra
meaning that comes in when a sentence, in addition to making a statement, is meant to be insulting,
or flattering, or is interpreted so — we may call it
emotive meaning — is not so different from plain

statement as we are apt to suppose. As the word means the missing part of its contexts and is a substitute for them, so the insulting intention may be the substitute for a kick,—the missing part of its context. The same general theorem covers all the modes of meaning.

I began tonight by speaking of the poaching of the other language functions on the preserve of pure exposition. Pure exposition has its guardian passions no doubt — though I do not know their names. But they are not often as strong as the poachers and are easily beguiled by them. It has been so necessary to us, especially since the physical basis of civilization became technical, to care at least sometimes for the truth only and keep the poachers sometimes out, that we have exaggerated enormously the extent of pure exposition. It is a relatively rare occurrence outside the routine of train services and the tamer, more settled parts of the sciences. We have exaggerated our success for strategic reasons — some of them good, because encouraging, if we do not too much hoodwink ourselves. I have aimed at points tonight to be merely expository in my remarks, but I know better than to suppose I have succeeded. We shall find, preëminently in the subject of rhetoric, that interpretations and opinions about interpretations that are not primarily steps of partisan policy are excessively hard to arrive at. And thereby we re-discover that the world — so far from being a solid matter of fact — is rather a fabric of conventions, which for obscure reasons it has

suited us in the past to manufacture and support.
And that sometimes is a dismaying re-discovery
which seems to unsettle our foundations.

Anyone who publishes a book with the word
'Meaning' in its title becomes the recipient of a fan-
mail of peculiar character. In comes a dribble of
letters ever after from people who are quite un-
mistakably lunatics. Indeed, it seems that the subject is a dangerous one. Intense preoccupation with
the sources of our meanings is disturbing, increasing
our sense that our beliefs are a veil and an artificial
veil between ourselves and something that otherwise than through a veil we cannot know. Something of the same sort can happen in travel. Anyone
who has visited a sufficiently strange country and
come into close contact with its life knows how un-
settling and disorientating is the recognition of the
place of conventions in our mental world. And the
effect is deeper as the contact is closer. Few men
have come into closer and more active contact with
an alien world than Colonel Lawrence and when, at
the end of the Introduction to *The Seven Pillars of
Wisdom,* he writes of the selves which converse in the
void, he says, "Then madness was very near, as I believe it would be near the man who could see things
through the veils at once of two customs, two educa-
tions, two environments." He is writing of fatigue,
and the page reeks of the extremities of war and of
the desert — the desert which pushes man down to
the limits of his endurance. The meditation of a
single code of meanings is not so devastating, and I

have seen already enough of Bryn Mawr to realize that it bears no least resemblance to a desert. We may then continue undeterred by the implications of my fan-mail.

The subject of the next lecture will be the Doctrine of Usage and the Interinanimation of Words and, as the rest of the course will be literary rather than philosophical and will attempt rather to practise than to theorize, I may close here with some lines from George Chapman about the theoretic principles of Rhetoric, the conduct of interpretation and "impartial contention" and their proper relation to action. It comes in a poem entitled

To Young Imaginaries in Knowledge.

> This rather were the way, if thou wouldst be
> A true proficient in philosophy
> Dissemble what thou studiest until
> By thy impartial contention
> Thou provest thee fit to do as to profess
> And if thou still profess it not, what less
> Is thy philosophy if in thy deeds
> Rather than signs and shadows, it proceeds.

I must apologize if in this Lecture I have departed from the spirit of his recommendation.

LECTURE III

THE INTERINANIMATION OF WORDS

Since children learn the use of words most evidently
without having any data or fixed points to go upon,
philosophers and candid persons may learn at last to
understand one another with facility and certainty.—
David Hartley, *On Man*.

LECTURE III

THE INTERINANIMATION OF WORDS

I TURN now to that other sense of 'context'—the literary context—which I distinguished last time from the technical sense of 'context,' as a recurrent group of events, that is convenient for the theorem of meaning. Let us consider some of the effects on words of their combination in sentences, and how their meaning depends upon the other words before and after them in the sentence. What happens when we try with a sentence to decide what single words in it mean?

The sentence, of course, as Aristotle taught, is the unit of discourse. We can hardly give too much importance here to the influence of our modern way of separating words in writing. In conversation we do not ordinarily separate them so—unless we are asking questions about words. With languages which have not been used in writing and thus subjected to a special kind of grammatical analysis—it is worth recalling that grammar takes its name from writing—there is often very great uncertainty as to where one word ends and another begins. The written form gives words far more independence than they possess as units of sound in speech and we derive thence a habit of supposing that they have far more independence as regards their meanings than they usually have in either written or spoken discourse.

The mutual dependence of words varies evidently with the type of discourse. At one end of the scale, in the strict exposition of some highly criticized and settled science through technicalized and rigid speech, a large proportion of them are independent. They mean the same whatever other words they are put with ; or if a word fluctuates, it moves only into a small number of stable positions, which can be recorded and are anchored to definitions. That is the ideal limit towards which we aim in exposition. Unfortunately we tend — increasingly since the 17th Century — to take rigid discourse as the norm, and impose its standards upon the rest of speech. This is much as if we thought that water, for all its virtues, in canals, baths and turbines, were really a weak form of ice. The other end of the scale is in poetry — in some forms of poetry rather. We know very much less about the behavior of words in these cases — when their virtue is to have no fixed and settled meaning separable from those of the other words they occur with. There are many more possibilities here than the theory of language has yet tried to think out. Often the whole utterance in which the co-operating meanings of the component words hang on one another is not itself stable in meaning. It utters not one meaning but a *movement* among meanings. Of course, even in the strictest prose we always have one thing that may be described as a movement of meaning.   We have change as the sentence develops. In "The cat is on the mat" we begin with the cat and end with the mat.   There is a progression of some sort in every explicit sentence.   But in the strictest prose the meanings of the separate words theoretically stay put and thought passes from one to another of them.   At the other end of the scale the whole meaning of the sentence shifts, and with it any meanings we may try to ascribe to the individual words.   In the extreme case it will go on moving as long as we bring fresh wits to study it. When Octavius Cæsar is gazing down at Cleopatra dead, he says,

> She looks like sleep,
> As she would catch another Antony
> In her strong toil of grace.

"Her strong toil of grace."   Where, in terms of what entries in what possible dictionary, do the meanings here of *toil* and *grace* come to rest?

But my subject is Rhetoric rather than Poetics and I want to keep to prose which is not too far from the strict scientific or 'rigid' end of this scale of dependent variabilities.   In the kind of prose I am talking now, you have usually to wait till I have gone on a bit before you can decide how you will understand the opening parts of the sentences.   If, instead, I were reading you the first few theorems of Euclid, that would not be so.   You would understand, as soon as I said 'a triangle,' what the word meant, and though what I went on to say might qualify the meaning ('having two sides equal'), it would not destroy or completely change the meaning that you had so far given to the word. But in most prose, and more than we ordinarily suppose, the opening words have to wait for those that follow to settle what they shall mean — if indeed that ever gets settled.

All this holds good not only as to the *sense* of the waiting words but as regards all the other functions of language which we can distinguish and set over against the mere sense. It holds for the *feeling* if any towards what I am talking about, for *the relation towards my audience* I want to establish or maintain with the remark, and for the *confidence* I have in the soundness of the remark — to mention three main sorts of these other language functions. In speech, of course, I have the aid of intonation for these purposes. But, as with the meanings of words, so with the intonation structure. The intonation of the opening words is likely to be ambiguous; it waits till the utterance is completed for its full interpretation.

In writing we have to replace intonation as far as we can. Most of the more recondite virtues of prose style come from the skill with which the rival claims of these various language functions are reconciled and combined. And many of the rather mysterious terms that are usually employed in discussing these matters, *harmony, rhythm, grace, texture, smoothness, suppleness, impressiveness,* and so on are best taken up for analysis from this point of

view. Or rather the passages which seem to exemplify these qualities (or fail to) are best exam-
ined with the multiplicity of the language functions
in mind. For we can obviously do nothing with such
words as these by themselves, in the blue. They may
mean all sorts of different things in different literary
contexts.

I have been leading up—or down, if you like—
to an extremely simple and obvious but fundamental remark : that no word can be judged as to
whether it is good or bad, correct or incorrect,
beautiful or ugly, or anything else that matters to
a writer, in isolation. That seems so evident that I
am almost ashamed to say it, and yet it flies straight
in the face of the only doctrine that for two hundred
years has been officially inculcated—when any doctrine is inculcated in these matters. I mean the
doctrine of Usage. The doctrine that there is a
right or a good use for every word and that literary
virtue consists in making that good use of it.

There are several bones that can be picked with
that doctrine—as it has been expounded in many
epochs and, in particular for us, from the middle
of the 18th Century onwards. It is the worst legacy
we have from that, in other ways, happy Century.
At its best it can be found in George Campbell's
Philosophy of Rhetoric—otherwise an excellent
book in many respects. At its worst, or nearly its
worst, the doctrine can be found in most of the
Manuals of Rhetoric and Composition which have
afflicted the schools—American schools especially.

It asserts that "Good use is the general, present-day practice of the best writers." One bone we could pick would be with that 'best.' How are they the best writers except by using the words in the best ways? We settle that they *are* the best writers because we find them using their words successfully. We do not settle that theirs is the right, the 'good usage' of the words because *they* use them so. Never was there a crazier case of putting the cart before the horse. It is as though we were to maintain that apples are healthy because * wise people eat them, instead of recognizing that it is the other way about — that it is what the food will do for us which makes us eat it, not the fact that we eat it which makes it good food.

But that is not the main bone I have to pick with the doctrine, which is that it blanks out and hides the interinanimation between words. I had better cite you a sentence or two in evidence, or you may think I am inventing a ghost to exorcize. I will take them from a *Manual of Rhetoric* which carries the names of three authors : Messrs. Gardiner, Kittredge and Arnold. And I choose this book because the regard which I have for Mr. Kittredge's name makes a doctrine which has that sanction seem the better worth refuting. The authors write : "Usage governs language. There is no other standard. By usage, however, is meant the practice of the best writers and speakers." (I have already asked what

---

* 'Because' is offering to play one of its most troublesome tricks here, of course, in the shift from 'cause' to 'reason.'

standard is supposed to settle which are the best.)
They go on to consider "four great general principles of choice : *correctness, precision, appropriate-
ness* and *expressiveness,*" which, they say, "within
the limits of good usage and in every case controlled
by it . . . should guide us in the choice of words."
And this is what they say of correctness : "Correctness is the most elementary of all requirements.
The meanings of words are settled by usage. If we
use a word incorrectly — that is in a sense which
does not customarily belong to it — our readers will
miss our thought, or, at best, they must arrive at it
by inference and guesswork."

Inference and guesswork! What else is interpretation? How, apart from inference and skilled
guesswork, can we be supposed ever to understand
a writer or speaker's thought? This is, I think, a
fine case of poking the fire from the top. But I
have still my main bit of evidence to give you. My
authors say : "In studying the four great principles
of choice, we observe that only the first (correctness) involves the question of right and wrong.
The others deal with questions of discrimination
between better and worse — that is with the closer
adaptation of words to the thoughts and feelings
which we undertake to express. Further, it is only
in dealing with the first principle (correctness) that
we can keep our attention entirely on the single
word."

There ! that is the view I wished to illustrate. Let
us not boggle about the oddities of its expression :

'right and wrong,' 'better and worse'; or worry as
to how by keeping "our attention entirely on a single
word" we could settle anything at all about it —
except perhaps about its spelling! The important
point is that words are here supposed just sheerly
to possess their sense, as men have their names in the
reverse case, and to carry this meaning with them
into sentences regardless of the neighbour words.
That is the assumption I am attacking, because, if
we follow up its practical consequences in writing
and reading and trace its effects upon interpretation, we shall find among them no small proportion
of the total of our verbal misunderstandings.

I am anxious not to seem to be illustrating this
sort of misunderstanding myself here, unwittingly,
in my interpretation of this passage. I know well
enough that the authors probably had in mind such
incorrectness as occurs when people say 'ingenious'
when they mean 'ingenuous'; and I know that the
Usage Doctrine can be interpreted in several ways
which make it true and innocuous.

It can say and truly, for example, that we learn
how to use words from responding to them and
noting how other people use them. Just how we do
so learn is a deep but explorable question. It can
say equally truly, that a general conformity between
users is a condition of communication. *That* no
one would dream of disputing. But if we consider
conformity we see that there are two kinds of conformity. Conformity in the general process of interpretation, and conformity in the specific products.

We all know how the duller critics of the 18th Century (the century that gave us the current Doctrine of Usage) the people Wordsworth was thinking of when he wrote his Preface, confused the poetic product with the poetic process and thought a poem good because it used poetic diction — the words that former good poets had used — and used them in the same ways.   The Usage Doctrine, in the noxious interpretation of it, is just that blunder in a more pervasive and more dangerous incidence.   The noxious interpretation is the common one.   Its evil is that it takes the senses of an author's words to be things we know before we read him, fixed factors with which he has to build up the meaning of his sentences as a mosaic is put together of discrete independent tesserae.   Instead, they are resultants which we arrive at only through the interplay of the interpretative possibilities of the whole utterance.   In brief, we have to guess them and we guess much better when we realize we are guessing, and watch out for indications, than when we think we know.*

There are as many morals for the writer as for the reader in all this, but I will keep to interpretation.   A word or phrase when isolated momentarily from its controlling neighbours is free to develop irrelevant senses which may then beguile half the other words to follow it.   And this is at least equally true with the language functions *other than sense,* with *feeling,* say.   I will give you one example of

* See the Note at the end of this Lecture.

an erratic interpretation of feeling, and if I take it from the same *Manual of Rhetoric* that is because it illustrates one of the things to which the mosaic view or habit of interpretation, as opposed to the organic, often leads.

The Authors give the following from Bacon's *Advancement of Learning*. And in re-reading it I will ask you to note how cunningly Bacon, in describing some misuses of learning, takes back with one hand what he seems to be offering with the other, indicating both why men do prefer misuses and why they should not do so.

> But the greatest error of all the rest is the mistaking or misplacing of the last or furthest end of knowledge. For men have entered into a desire of learning and knowledge, sometimes upon a natural curiosity and inquisitive appetite; sometimes to entertain their minds with variety and delight; sometimes for ornament and reputation; and sometimes to enable them to victory of wit and contradiction; and most times for lucre and profession; and seldom sincerely to give a true account of their gift of reason, to the benefit and use of men: as if there were sought in knowledge a couch, whereupon to rest a searching or restless spirit; or a terrace, for a wandering and variable mind to walk up and down with a fair prospect; or a tower of state, for a proud mind to raise itself upon; or a fort or commanding ground, for strife and contention; or a shop, for profit or sale; and not a rich storehouse, for the glory of the Creator and the relief of man's estate.

There is much to take to heart here — especially as to the couch aspect of the Usage Doctrine, and, I must admit, the tower and the fort — but what the authors say about it is this:

Here the splendor of the imagery is no mere embellishment. Without it, Bacon could not have given
adequate expression to his enthusiastic appreciation of
learning and his fine scorn for the unworthy uses to
which it is sometimes put. At the same time, the figures elevate the passage from the ordinary levels of
prose to a noble eloquence. (p. 372)

What splendor is there in the imagery? These
images have no splendor as Bacon uses them, but are
severely efficient, a compact means for saying what
he has to say. His 'enthusiastic appreciation' (a
poor phrase, I suggest, to smudge over him!) of the
use of knowledge and his 'fine scorn' of unworthy
uses are given only if we refuse to be beguiled by
the possibilities of splendor in the isolated images.
Loose them even a little from their service, let their
'splendor' act independently, and they begin at once
to fight against his intention. For the terrace, the
tower and the fort, if they were allowed to 'elevate,'
would make the misplacings of the last and furthest
end of knowledge seem much grander than "a true
account of their gift of reason, to the benefit and use
of men"—as a terrace or tower of state or a fort will
seem grander than a mere rich storehouse.

Let me go on to some further types of the mutual
control and interinanimation between words. So
far I have considered only the influence of words actually present in the passage, but we have to include
words which are not actually being uttered and are
only in the background. Take the case of what are
variously called expressive, symbolic, or simulative

words — words which 'somehow illustrate the meaning more immediately than do ordinary speech forms,' to quote Leonard Bloomfield.   Examples are *flip, flap, flop, flitter, flimmer, flicker, flutter, flash, flush, flare, glare, glitter, glow, gloat, glimmer, bang, bump, lump, thump, thwack, whack, sniff, sniffle, snuff.* . . Why should these seem so peculiarly appropriate, or fitting, to the meanings we use them for?   The popular view is that these words just simply imitate, are copies of, what they mean.   But that is a short-cut theory which often does not work, and we can, I think, go further and do better.   As Bloomfield, in his excellent book, *Language,* says, "the explanation is a matter of grammatical structure, to the speaker it seems as if the sounds were especially suited to the meaning."   The speaker usually thinks moreover that the word seems suited because in some way it resembles the meaning, or, if this seems unplausible, that there must be *some* direct connection between them.   If it is not the sound of the word which resembles the meaning then perhaps the tongue and lip movements instead imitate something to do with the meaning and so on.   Sir Richard Paget's theories of imitative gestures are likely to be appealed to nowadays.

The most that the modern linguist — who compares the very different words which are used in different languages for their meanings — is prepared to allow towards this resemblance of sound and sense is that "we can distinguish, with various degrees of clearness and with doubtful cases on the border line, a system of initial and final root-forming morphemes of vague signification." Note how guarded Bloomfield is over such a point.

I must explain what a morpheme is. Two or more words are said to share a morpheme when they have, at the same time, something in common in their meaning and something in common in their sound. The joint semantic-phonetic unit which distinguishes them is what is called a morpheme. It is the togetherness of a peculiar sound and a peculiar meaning for a number of words.

Thus *flash, flare, flame, flicker, flimmer* have in common the sound (fl-) and a suggestion of a 'moving light'—and this joint possession is the morpheme. Similarly *blare, flare, glare, stare* have the sound (-eə) in common and also the meaning 'big light or noise' shall we say, and this couple—sound and meaning is the morpheme. So with 'smoothly wet' and (sl-) in *slime, slip, slush, slobber, slide, slither.* But *pare, pear, pair,* though they have a sound in common, have no meaning in common, so have no common morpheme.

Of course, the existence of a group of words with a common morpheme has an influence on the formation of other words, and on the pronunciation of other words—assimilating them to the group. Thus, given *skid* and *skate,* that is a strong additional reason, against an English convention, for saying *skee* rather than *shee.*

This pedantic looking term, *morpheme,* is useful because with its help we manage to avoid saying that the sound (sl-) somehow itself means something like 'smoothly wet or slippery' and gain a way of saying no more than that a group of words which share that sound also share a peculiar meaning. And that is all we are entitled to say.   To go further and say that the words share the meaning *because* they contain this sound and because this sound has that meaning is to bring in more than we know — an explanation or theory to account for what we do know.   And actually it is a bad explanation.   For this sound, by itself, means nothing.   It is not the shared sound but each of the words which has the meaning.   The sound by itself either means nothing at all — as with (fl) in *flame, flare, flash, flicker* — or as with (-ɛə) in *blare, flare, glare, stare* it has by itself only an irrelevant meaning, namely, that of *air,* 'what we breathe.'

The theoretical position here is worth close study because it is typical of a very large group of positions in which we tend, too boldly and too innocently, to go beyond our evidence and to assume, as the obvious explanation, as almost a datum, what is really the conclusion of a vague and quick and unchecked inductive argument, often a bad and unwarrantable argument.   Why should a group of words with a sound in common have similar meanings unless there was a correspondence of some kind between the sound and the meaning?   That seems plausible.   But state the argument more explicitly, look over the evidence carefully, and it becomes unplausible, for then we have to notice the other words which share the sound but do not share the meaning and the other words which share the meaning without the sound. Then we see that we have been applying to words the sort of argument which would represent a fashion as a spontaneous expression of original taste on the part of all who follow it. We find in fact that we have been looking at the problem upside down. That so far from a perceived correspondence between sound and meaning being the explanation of the sharing, the existence of a group of words with a common sound and meaning is the explanation of our belief in a correspondence.

This situation, I said a moment ago, is typical. We can hardly, I think, exaggerate in an estimate of the number of literary and rhetorical problems which, as usually formulated, are upside down in this fashion. For example, our common assumption that when a word such as *beautiful* or *art* or *religion* or *good,* is used in a great variety of ways, there will be found something in common to all the uses, something which is the fundamental or essential meaning of the word and the explanation of its use. So we spend our wits trying to discover this common essential meaning, without considering that we are looking for it, most often, only as a result of a weak and hasty inductive argument. This assumption that the same word ought to have or must have the same meaning, in an important respect, is one of those bullying assumptions that the context theorem of meanings would defend us from — in the way I discussed in my lecture last week,

But to come back to this parallel assumption that some words, apart from other words, and in their own right in virtue of their sound must mean certain things. It was Aristotle who said that there can be no natural connection between the sound of any language and the things signified, and, if we set the problem right side up and remember the other words before examining it, we shall have to agree with him. Indeed, if we ask the question fairly it becomes — when we get it clear — nearly senseless. What resemblance or natural connection can there be between the semantic and phonetic elements in the morpheme? One is a sound, the other a reference. 'Is (fl-) really like 'moving light' in any way in which (sl-) or (gl-) is not?' Is that not like asking whether the taste of turkey is like growing in some way that the taste of mint is not?

I conclude then that these expressive or symbolic words get their feeling of being peculiarly fitting from the other words sharing the morpheme which support them in the background of the mind. If that is so, all sorts of consequences are at once evident. In translation, for example, the expressive word in another language will not necessarily sound at all like the original word. It will be a word that is backed up by other words in a somewhat analogous fashion. Evidently again, a proper appreciation of the expressiveness of a word in a foreign language will be no matter of merely knowing its meaning and relishing its sound. It is a matter of having, in the background of the mind, the other words in the language which share morphemes with it. Thus no one can appreciate these expressive features of foreign words justly without a really wide familiarity with the language. Without that our estimates are merely whimsical.

We can, and I think should, extend this notion of a word as being backed up by other words that are not uttered or thought of. A first extension is to words that sound alike but do not share a morpheme, do not have a common meaning but only some relevant meaning. Thus *blare, scare* and *dare* do not share a morpheme, but on occasion the peculiar force of *blare* may well come to it in part from the others. This, of course, is only recognizing on a larger, wider scale the principle that Lewis Carroll was using in Jabberwocky. Its relevance to the theory of rhymes and assonances is obvious.

Another and a wider extension would include not only influences from words which in part sound alike, but from other words which in part overlap in meaning. Words, for example, which we might have used instead, and, together with these, the reasons why we did not use them. Another such extension looks to the other uses, in other contexts, of what we, too simply, call 'the same word.' The meaning of a word on some occasions is quite as much in what it keeps out, or at a distance, as in what it brings in. And, on other occasions, the meaning comes from other partly parallel uses whose relevance we can feel, without necessarily being able to state it explicitly. But with these last leaps I may seem in danger of making the force of a word, the feeling that no other word could possibly do so well or take its place, a matter whose explanation will drag in the whole of the rest of the language. I am not sure, though, that we need be shy of something very like this as a conclusion. A really masterly use of a language — in free or fluid, not technical discourse — Shakespeare's use of English for example, goes a long way towards using the language as a whole.

Cleopatra, taking up the asp, says to it :

> Come, thou mortal wretch,
> With thy sharp teeth this knot intrinsicate
> Of life at once untie ; poor venomous fool,
> Be angry, and despatch !

Consider how many senses of *mortal,* besides 'death-dealing' come in ; compare : 'I have immortal longings in me.'   Consider *knot :* 'This knot intrinsicate of life': 'Something to be undone,' 'Something that troubles us until it is undone,' 'Something by which all holding-together hangs,' 'The nexus of all meaning.'   Whether the homophone *not* enters in here may be thought a doubtful matter.   I feel it does. But consider *intrinsicate* along with *knot.*   Edward Dowden, following the fashion of his time in making Shakespeare as simple as possible, gives 'intricate' as the meaning here of *intrinsicate.*   And the Oxford Dictionary, sad to say, does likewise.   But Shakespeare is bringing together half a dozen meanings from *intrinsic* and *intrinse :* 'Familiar,' 'intimate,' 'secret,' 'private,' 'innermost,' 'essential,' 'that which constitutes the very nature and being of a thing'—all the medical and philosophic meanings of his time as well as 'intricate' and 'involved.' What the word does is exhausted by no one of these meanings and its force comes from all of them and more. As the movement of my hand uses nearly the whole skeletal system of the muscles and is supported by them, so a phrase may take its powers from an immense system of supporting uses of other words in other contexts.

NOTE

The word *usage* itself well illustrates some of the more troublesome shifts of meaning.   An improved Rhetoric has among its aims an improved control over these.   Here perhaps a list of some of the senses of *usage* may help us in avoiding misunderstanding.

(1) The most inclusive sense is "the entire range of the powers which the word can exert as an instrument of communication in all situations and in co-operation with any other words."
(In this sense 'Usage, and usage alone, undoubtedly controls language.')

(2) "Some specific power which, in a limited range of situations and with a limited type of verbal context the word normally exerts."
(This is often called a *use* or *sense* and is what the Dictionary attempts to record in its definitions, by giving other words, phrases and sentences with the same specific power.)

(3) An instance of 2, at a certain place in Shakespeare, say, which may be appealed to to show that the word can have that power.

(4) A supposed fixed 'proper' meaning that the word must be kept to (has in its own right, etc.)   This

notion is derived from 1, 2 and 3 by over-simplification and a misconception of the working of language which, typically, takes the meaning of a sentence to be something built up from separate meanings of its words — instead of recognizing that it is the other way about and that the meanings of words are derived from the meanings of sentences in which they occur. This misconception assimilates the process by which words have their meanings determined with that by which they have their spelling determined and is the origin of a large part of misinterpretation.

LECTURE IV
SOME CRITERIA OF WORDS

There is no warrant for the placing on these inevitably rather light heads and hearts, on any company of you, assaulted, in our vast vague order, by many pressing wonderments, the *whole* of the burden of a care for tone.—Henry James, *The Question of our Speech*.

LECTURE IV

SOME CRITERIA OF WORDS

LAST week I was concerned with the interdependences of words in discourse, and the interinanimation between them. I began by arraigning the conventional Doctrine of Usage. I accused it of forgetting that a word is always a cooperative member of an organism, the utterance, and therefore cannot properly — in ordinary free, fluid, non-technical discourse — be thought to have a meaning of its own, a fixed correct usage, or even a small limited number of correct usages unless by 'usage' we mean the whole *how* of its successful cooperations with other words, the entire range of the varied powers which, with their aid, it can exert. The traditional Usage Doctrine, I said, treated language on the bad analogy of a mosaic, and conceived composition and interpretation as though they were a putting together or taking apart of pieces with a fixed shape and color, whereas, in fact, the interinanimation of the meanings of words is at least as great as in any other mode of mental performance. A note in a musical phrase takes its character from, and makes its contribution only with, the other notes about it; a seen color is only what it is with respect to the other colors co-present with it in the visual field; the seen size or distance of an object

69

is interpreted only with regard to the other things seen with it. Everywhere in perception we see this interinanimation (or interpenetration as Bergson used to call it). So with words, too, but much more ; the meaning we find for a word comes to it only with respect to the meanings of the other words we take with it. And towards the end of the lecture I extended this view to include not only the other words uttered with it, but also *unuttered* words in various relations to it which may be backing it up though we never think of them. So, in perceiving the size or shape or distance of a thing, all sorts of actions we might take in walking towards it, or grasping it, come in — though we may never think of them — to guide our interpretation. Again, the etymological hint of *inter* sums up the whole story.

I want now to touch upon two or three considerations which support and illustrate this view before proceeding to discuss some of the criteria, or headings, under which we commonly profess to judge the merits or demerits of words. You will see, I hope, that these criteria — *precision, vividness, expressiveness, clarity, beauty,* are representative instances of them — are misleading and unprofitable to study unless we use them with a due recognition of this interdependence among the words we use them to describe and an alert distrust of our habit of taking words and their meanings for examination in isolation. The isolation is never complete, of course ; a completely isolated word would be meaningless. The detachment we attempt is by means of a supposed standard setting, an imaginary, schematic context which is assumed to be representative. And it is the habit of trusting such supplied but unexamined contexts ('as generally used,' 'in ordinary discourse,' 'in common parlance' and so on) that I am attacking. The strength of this habit is too great for anyone once for all, or for long at a time, to rid himself of it. The view that meanings belong to words in their own right — and the more sophisticated views which have the same effect — are a branch of sorcery, a relic of the magical theory of names. And my experience is that the most determined efforts do no more than free us from it now and then for a few precious moments. Thus in exhorting you to discard it, I feel in the position of that Basuto Chief, reported by Casalis in 1861, who called his tribe together to warn them against another mode of sorcery. "Sorcery," said the Basuto Chief — who was evidently as much persuading himself as them —"Sorcery only exists in the mouths of those who speak it. It is no more in the power of a man to kill his fellow by mere effort of his will, than it would be to raise him from the dead. That is my opinion. Nevertheless, you sorcerers who hear me speak, use moderation!"

So here, though I may be intellectually persuaded, and persuade you, that a word by itself without a setting of other words, uttered or supplied, can no more have a meaning than a patch of color can have a size or distance without its setting, yet I do not expect that our behavior will be much changed. The habitual pull of the contrary received assumption is too strong. Our best hope is that we may learn to use moderation in our reliance on that assumption.

The evil influence of the assumption is most glaringly shown with the abstract words upon which all discussions of general theoretical topics turn. Outside of the sciences — in our talk about politics, society or conduct, or about science itself, in all branches of philosophy including psychology, in all discussions of art, literature, language, truth, beauty and the good, our principal terms incessantly change their meanings with the sentences they go into and the contexts they derive from. We are all ready enough to suspect this, if not in our own talk at least in that of our fellows, and ready to see in it a chief cause for the lamented fact that these subjects show — once we have allowed for current fashions — strangely little progress. But both the extent *and the plan* of these deluding shifts are hidden from us by the assumption I am attacking. It leads us to think that a shift of meaning is a flaw in discourse, a regrettable accident, instead of a virtue. And therefore we neglect to study the plan of the shifts.

The assumption is that words have, or should have, proper meanings which people should recognize, agree about and stick to. A pretty program, if it were possible. But, outside the technical languages of the sciences, it is not possible. For in the topics with which all generally interesting discussion is concerned, words must shift their meanings thus. Without these shifts such mutual understanding as we achieve would fail even within the narrowed resultant scope. Language, losing its subtlety with its suppleness, would lose also its power to serve us.

The remedy is not to resist these shifts but to learn to follow them. They recur in the same forms with different words; they have similar plans and common patterns, which experience enables us to observe and obey in practice — sometimes with a skilful ease which seems amazing when we examine it. We may reasonably hope that systematic study will in time permit us to compare, describe and explain these systematic ambiguity or transference patterns on a scale as much surpassing our best present-day Dictionary Technique as, say, our present competence in chemistry surpasses that of Bacon who foresaw it. Even now, if we could take *systematic* cognizance of even a small part of the shifts we fleetingly observe, the effect would be like that of introducing the multiplication table to calculators who just happened to know the working of a few sums and no others. And with such a clarification, such a translation of our skills into comprehension, a new era of human understanding and co-operation in thinking would be at hand. It would not be difficult to do not a little towards this at once. What stands in the way is chiefly the Proper Meaning Superstition and the effort it sustains towards increased rigidity in fields where rigidity is inappropriate.

These shifts deceive us most when they affect abstract words, because then they are hardest to follow. But they occur as much and as variously with seemingly simple concrete words. With these we often follow them so easily that we may not suspect that any shifts are taking place. The word *book*, for example, troubles no one. And yet compare the use of *book*, in which we distinguish a book from a magazine or journal, with that in which a majority of speakers in England (call them uneducated if you like) describe a weekly as a book. Or compare the senses of *book* in "It's a formidable volume, but it's not a book." "He has his mind full of his book." "Writing a book." "Binding a book." "Printing a book." "Rearranging the books in the catalogue." In each of these we have shifted the sense of *book*, sometimes to positions incompatible with one another. No one, for example, will ever bind the book which I am now making of these lectures. What will be printed and what will be bound are different things altogether from what I am now working on (a set of ideas), though of course they are connected in obvious ways with it.

We follow these shifts without trouble because we are familiar with them. We are not yet so familiar with the shifts of the more heavily worked abstract words of reflection. It is the hope and the great opportunity for intellectual improvement that we may in time become equally familiar with them. That, I would say, is fundamentally the aim and the justification of advanced verbal education, a thing

otherwise often hard to justify; and the best answer to the troublesome question, "Why should we
worry ourselves with it?" is that thereby we may
better find out what we and others are thinking.

Towards the end of the last lecture I was suggesting that our words commonly take meaning through
the influence of other words which we may never
think of but which in the back of the mind co-operate in controlling them. And I concluded with the
remark that a great writer often gains his aim by
making a single phrase pull with or against large
ranges of the language. This, if true, is, of course,
an additional argument against the Proper Usage Superstition. We can say of the single word what
Donne said of single sentences, "Sentences in Scrip-
ture, like hairs in horsetails, concur in one root of
beauty and strength; but being plucked out one by
one, serve only for springes and snares." We need
especially to beware of plucking words out one by
one when we are tempted to judge new additions
that are being made to the language, for these are
more easily detached and carry less latent, or assumed context with them. Nothing better tests
our ideas about the choice of words than the reasons we find ourselves giving for liking or disliking
a new word and nothing better exposes the doctrine
of usage. Our language is growing faster and in
more varied ways than at any time since Elizabeth's.
It is estimated that even for that conservative sec-
tion of the English speaking peoples which lives in

England, as many as thirty new words a year have recently been coming into general use. This quite apart from the technicalities of the trades and the sciences. A large number of them crossed the Atlantic and it is fair to say, I think, that among these will be found many that have been most heartily welcomed in England.

But new words are not always or even usually welcomed, certainly not by the vocal few who profess to have explicit reasons for their opinions about them. A new word commonly stirs up complaints and some of these complaints are worth study for the interesting light they throw upon current assumptions about language.

Let me take first the complaints most often heard against the new words that are coined in the sciences — against those of them that pass from scientific use into general currency. These complaints are, commonly, that they are awkward or difficult to pronounce or too long, and that they are not labels but compacted descriptions or explanations. The prejudice is sometimes so strong that even the lexicographers succumb to it. You will not find, in the two-volume *Shorter Oxford Dictionary,* for example, either the word extraversion (extravert) or introversion (introvert) in their Jungian senses — indispensable though these words have been to an enormous amount of conversation.

Now what do these complaints amount to? What sort of case can be made out for them? First as to the awkwardness — the uncertainty that may be felt as to how to pronounce them, as to whether, for example, *epistemology* should be *e'pistemology, epis'-temology, episte'mology* or *epistemol'ogy*. Sir James Murray in his Preface to the *Oxford Dictionary*, notes that, on applying "directly to the introducer of a word, to know how he pronounces it, or means it to be pronounced," on several occasions, the answer received was "that he has never thought of its pronunciation, does not presume to say how it ought to be pronounced, and leaves it to people to pronounce as they like, or to the DICTIONARY to say what is the *right* pronunciation."

This, Sir James complained, inverts the established order by which speech comes first. But surely the surprised introducers were justified. Being themselves the very fountain-heads of usage they knew better than to trust it! They knew that the good and bad of words have other standards. How a word should be pronounced is, at least in part, a matter requiring reference to how the other words in the language are pronounced. And that evidently is the lexicographer's not the philosopher's or the psychologist's business. But unfortunately the lexicographer is sometimes himself — in these matters of pronunciation as in matters of interpretation — too much under the spell of crude usage theories. Daunted by his responsibilities he falls back upon the task of making a phonetic record of pronunciations that have been established, or he takes refuge in a variety of the usage doctrine which I can ticket here as obedience to the Club Spirit.

This is an important mode of the usage doctrine. Essentially it makes the conduct of language subservient to manners — to the manners of a special set of speakers. If you belong to a certain sort of Club you thereby enter upon an engagement to behave, while there, in certain ways — or rather an engagement not to behave in certain other ways. As usual it is much easier to say what you will *not* do there, than what you will. Similarly, in using a language, you join a more or less select company — of correct users of the language. Deviation from their customs is *incorrectness* and is visited with a social penalty as such. And no account is taken, in this, of whether what you do is better or worse than the customs of the company. It is enough that it is different to bring you into condemnation.

This specialized form of control by usage, this social or snob control over all language, is obviously very wide and rigorous. One of the tasks of an improved Rhetoric is to question it, whether it concerns pronunciation or matters of meaning and interpretation. For the moment I am concerned with pronunciation, but I would like to insist that what I am saying about pronunciation has its parallels throughout the whole field and can be applied too to variations and specializations of meaning. Thus it was the Club Spirit in England which made us say "I'm sorry!" when you over here say "I beg your pardon!" Apart from the Club Spirit, your phrase is perhaps the better of the two, with less risk of confusing the important with the trivial. The effects of questioning the utility of the Rule of the Club Spirit would I believe be extremely drastic. The reasons for questioning it are, since it is itself a social rule, themselves social. In the past, I am willing to believe, such snob control was often useful to the whole community, not merely, as now, to the members of the Club, who find in it an advantage over their fellow citizens. This use of verbal differences as weapons in the class-war dates for us, in some important respects, from the 17th Century. In Shakespeare's age it seems probable that a less derogatory and a more humorous notice was taken of differences in speech. There was less need to be scornful. It was because a new stratification of society had arisen that the early 18th Century began to observe that niceties of pronunciation and expression constituted the most certain differentiation between a gentleman and his valet, between a lady and a mantua-maker. The new effort towards uniform spelling is another aspect of the same change. And it was then that a preoccupation with correctness (in this Club Spirit sense) became the obsession of the grammar-book merchants — of those (Steele is an example) who purveyed instruction to the new gentry about how they were to make it clear that they were really gentry.

That is the humiliating side of the Rule of the Club Spirit. But there is a worthier side. In the 18th Century — when comparatively few were educated, and when the education given was relatively all of a piece — this sort of correctness did give some reliable indication of culture in a deeper sense. Nowadays we educate a far larger proportion of a population ten times more numerous, and, what is more important, education in the humanities is no longer uniform. If asked for a definition of the humanities now, we would have to reply, "Anything that has anything to do with anything in the Metropolitan or the British Museums." And, with that, the Rule of the Club Spirit ceases to guarantee anything important about the depth of the culture of those who speak correctly or incorrectly, according or not according to its terms.

And yet how strong it still is. I suppose a large part of the justification of lectures in many colleges, is that they ensure that those who attend them will know how to pronounce the names of Italian painters and Greek heroines. Even extensive reading in prose translations of the classics will not protect us from the awful dangers of saying Saloam, or Pennylope or Hermy-one. I well remember a worthy young auto-didact from Manchester bursting in upon me to announce with deep enthusiasm that he had become, in the vacation, "Desperately keen on Dant and Goath." I do not believe that he would have read them with a whit more genuine profit had he known that he was really reading Dante and Goethe.

Enough about these breaches of the Club Spirit. Let us go back to the complaints against new scientific terms. 'Conciseness and pronunciability,' said Jeremy Bentham, are merits in a new-coined word.

A queer doctrine, we may think, to come from a man who, himself, for example, coined as key-terms in the analysis of metaphor — which he did so much to advance — the words *archetypation* and *phraseoplerosis :* for the discovery of the ground of the shift of meaning and the filling in of the phrase to represent that ground. How about conciseness as a merit? Must we not qualify it with that useful phrase 'other things being equal'? And shall we not then agree that, *with words,* other things are never equal and that very often length too (within limits) may be a merit in a word? Most especially when, as often with these scientific words, the meanings they have to carry are complex. It is an advantage with many scientific words that they should look scientific and should remind us that they belong to a system and depend upon assumptions which we must take account of. And there comes in the answer to that other complaint that so many of these words (*introversion* and *extraversion,* for example) are explanations, not labels. For familiar things, it is often said, we need a label, not a description. Yes! if the things are really familiar. But the dangers of mere labels when the things are not really familiar — of labels which give no hint of what they are attached to — should hardly need pointing out.

To pass to another type of complaint — that these words are cumbrous and ugly in themselves. I have seen it urged — and by no slight authority — that whereas good old words like *mind* and *thought* are neat, concise and beautiful, a word like *psychology* is cumbrous and disagreeable. How sound a complaint is that? And is it really a complaint against the form of the word or against some of its uses? Let us grant that some of the derivative uses of *psychology* are objectionable — because inconveniently and unnecessarily ambiguous — as when someone persists in talking and writing of *Shakespeare's psychology* without letting us see whether he means (1) Shakespeare's theories, if any, about the mind, (2) the assumptions Shakespeare unconsciously made about mental processes, (3) the inference as to mental processes we might arrive at from Shakespeare's work, or (4) (to go no further into these possibilities) just the way Shakespeare's own mind worked. These vagaries of the word are typical and unfortunate. They endanger discourse, and much use of that sort of language rightly discredits a speaker or writer. But such uses of *psychology* are no ground for complaint against the word in its use for the theoretical study of how the mind works, or in derivative uses where the context takes care of them. The complaint against *Shakespeare's psychology* is really against the inadequate contextual control. And for controlled uses of the word — seeing what a cumbrous subject psychology is — a cumbrous word may have therein its recommendation.

Such a word may, however, be tainted, for many, even in its prime use, by its associations with unhappy uses. This is a common case — especially with new words — and, I think, instructive. It can be illustrated with *colorful*. A violent distaste for this word, as for *tasteful*, is prevalent in many circles in England. Colorful came in seemingly about 1890. On the principle that any stick will do to beat a dog with, all sorts of reasons are brought out to justify dislike for it. That it is a hybrid, that it is vulgar, that we do not say *soundful* or *lightful*, that if we use it we shall soon be using *lifeful* and *laughterful*, that we already have 'full of color' which does its work, and so on. None of these objections will bear examination. Our language has too many lusty and valuable hybrids in it already for that to matter (compare *beautiful* and *joyful* which would be equally hybrids). Most of the other objections are drawn from analogy and may fairly be met by pursuing the analogies further. You will see that in doing so we would be considering the same sorts of situations, in which a word is backed up by other words, that we considered with the morphemes last week and that the analogies which would matter would not be those that were only evident to the philologist but those actually operative, on occasion, in backing up or deflecting (i.e., steering) our use of the words.

The interesting objection, against such words as *colorful*, concerns vulgarity. It is an objection that many new words are open to because they are often taken up most readily by people the objectors like to describe so. Moreover, that a word should be popular is often the chief con-

dition for its admission into the language and
to some people *popular* means what *vulgar* means.
But a word like *colorful* can evidently be used in
many different ways with different meanings, and to
compare these is the way to judge it.   We would
not judge a quadruped without deciding whether
it is a horse or a dog.   So, we ought not to judge
a word without considering what sorts of uses it is
peculiarly suited to and without remembering that
a good ferret makes a bad rabbit.   What then are
the peculiar utilities of the word *colorful?*

First, I would draw attention to the ironical implications it is capable of conveying.   Like the
phrases, *hard-working, painstaking, does his best,
industrious* and *well-intentioned,—* and others which
turn up in schoolmasters' reports, it can suggest
that if this is the best that can be said about something, well, we know where we are!   To call a
prose-style, or a dramatic production, *colorful* and
leave it at that, can be a very polite and therefore
very effective way of damning it with faint praise.
It is the more effective because it suggests that those
who will be content with it as straight praise are
not bringing a sufficient critical apparatus to bear
upon the matter.   There are, of course, uses of
colorful which have no such implications — where,
for example, that a thing should be full of color
is all we can ask, where no ironical reserves and no
disparagement can be intended.   And indeed it is
the fact that there are these other straight uses, and
that confusion between the straight and the derog-

atory uses is easy and frequent, that gives the word its peculiar subtlety on occasion.

And this confusion too is, I think, the source of the distaste for the word. If it is used straight, when the ironical implication would be in place, it suggests a lack of discrimination in the user, which — unless we analyse — we allow to infect the word itself. If *beautiful* were not such an old and well understood word we might let the same thing happen with it. Gross uses of *beautiful* might make the word itself a thing suited only to gross uses. When people talk of 'beautiful food' some are apt to shudder. When Mr. Eliot in *The Waste Land* makes one of his characters say,

> Well, that Sunday Albert was home, they had a hot
>   gammon,
> And they asked me in to get the beauty of it hot

he is using that shudder, and all the pathetic reverberations from its occasion and its contrasts. That is the full use of language — which dramatic writing more than any other, of course, requires. It takes its word, not as the repository of a single constant power but as a means by which the different powers it may exert in different situations are brought together and again with an interinanimating apposition.

I have taken *colorful* as a type word. Its own peculiar problems are local, perhaps temporary and unimportant — but if we pursue them we find that they lead us to most of the problems of the choice of words, and further still that they bring into view most of the problems of aesthetics. To realize that it is idle to ask of a word, "Is it beautiful?"—unless we are ready to ask thoroughly, "What will it do in its varied incidences?"—is a first step and a long step in the aesthetics of language. A parallel step must be made for every branch of aesthetics. A discussion of the reasons for the choice of words—which too often seems a trivial exchange of whimsies—can become an introduction to the theory of all choices. The art of so transforming it from a tea-table topic into the central discipline of education waits to be rediscovered, but the better we understand what place words hold in our lives the readier we shall be to admit that to think about their choice is the most convenient mode of thinking about the principle of all our choices.

LECTURE V

METAPHOR

Again, the more the mind knows, the better it understands its forces and the order of nature; the more it understands its forces or strength, the better it will be able to direct itself and lay down rules for itself; and the more it understands the order of nature, the more easily it will be able to liberate itself from useless things: of this, as we have said, consists the whole method.—Spinoza, *De intellectus emendatione.*

LECTURE V

METAPHOR

IT WAS Aristotle, no lesser man, who said, in *The Poetics,* "The greatest thing by far is to have a command of metaphor." But he went on to say, "This alone cannot be imparted to another: it is the mark of genius, for to make good metaphors implies an eye for resemblances." I do not know how much influence this remark has had: or whether it is at all responsible for our feeling that what it says is common-sense. But question it for a moment and we can discover in it, if we will to be malicious, here at the very beginning of the subject, the evil presence of three of the assumptions which have ever since prevented the study of this 'greatest thing by far' from taking the place it deserves among our studies and from advancing, as theory and practice, in the ways open to it.

One assumption is that 'an eye for resemblances' is a gift that some men have but others have not. But we all live, and speak, only through our eye for resemblances. Without it we should perish early. Though some may have better eyes than others, the differences between them are in degree only and may be remedied, certainly in some measure, as other differences are, by the right kinds of

89

teaching and study.   The second assumption denies this and holds that, though everything else may be taught, "This alone cannot be imparted to another." I cannot guess how seriously Aristotle meant this or what other subjects of teaching he had in mind as he spoke.   But, if we consider how we all of us attain what limited measure of a command of metaphor we possess, we shall see that no such contrast is valid.   As individuals we gain our command of metaphor just as we learn whatever else makes us distinctively human.   It is all imparted to us from others, with and through the language we learn, language which is utterly unable to aid us except through the command of metaphor which it gives. And that brings up the third and worst assumption — that metaphor is something special and exceptional in the use of language, a deviation from its normal mode of working, instead of the omnipresent principle of all its free action.

Throughout the history of Rhetoric, metaphor has been treated as a sort of happy extra trick with words, an opportunity to exploit the accidents of their versatility, something in place occasionally but requiring unusual skill and caution.   In brief, a grace or ornament or *added* power of language, not its constitutive form.   Sometimes, it is true, a writer will venture on speculations that go deeper.   I have just been echoing Shelley's observation that "Language is vitally metaphorical; that is, it marks the before unapprehended relations of things and perpetuates their apprehension, until words, which represent them, become, through time, signs for portions or classes of thought instead of pictures of integral thoughts : and then, if no new poets should arise to create afresh the associations which have been thus disorganised, language will be dead to all the nobler purposes of human intercourse." But that is an exceptional utterance and its implications have not yet been taken account of by rhetoricians. Nor have philosophers, as a body, done much better, though historians of language have long taught that we can find no word or description for any of the intellectual operations which, if its history is known, is not seen to have been taken, by metaphor, from a description of some physical happening. Only Jeremy Bentham, as successor to Bacon and Hobbes, insisted — with his technique of archetypation and phraseoplerosis — upon one inference that might be drawn ; namely, that the mind and all its doings are fictions. He left it to Coleridge, F. H. Bradley and Vaihinger to point to the further inference ; namely, that matter and its adventures, and all the derivative objects of contemplation, are fictions too, of varied rank because of varied service.

I have glanced for a moment at these deep waters into which a serious study of metaphor may plunge us, because possibly fear of them may be one cause why the study has so often not been enterprising and why Rhetoric traditionally has limited its inquiry to relatively superficial problems. But we shall not advance in even these surface problems unless we are ready to explore, as best we can, the depths of verbal interaction which give rise to them.

That metaphor is the omnipresent principle of language can be shown by mere observation. We cannot get through three sentences of ordinary fluid discourse without it, as you will be noticing throughout this lecture. Even in the rigid language of the settled sciences we do not eliminate or prevent it without great difficulty. In the semi-technicalised subjects, in aesthetics, politics, sociology, ethics, psychology, theory of language and so on, our constant chief difficulty is to discover how we are using it and how our supposedly fixed words are shifting their senses. In philosophy, above all, we can take no step safely without an unrelaxing awareness of the metaphors we, and our audience, may be employing; and though we may pretend to eschew them, we can attempt to do so only by detecting them. And this is the more true, the more severe and abstract the philosophy is. As it grows more abstract we think increasingly by means of metaphors that we profess *not* to be relying on. The metaphors we are avoiding steer our thought as much as those we accept. So it must be with any utterance for which it is less easy to know what we are saying than what we are not saying. And in philosophy, of which this is almost a definition, I would hold with Bradley that our pretence to do without metaphor is never more than a bluff waiting to be called. But if that is a truth, it is easier to utter than to accept with its consequences or to remember.

The view that metaphor is omnipresent in speech can be recommended theoretically. If you recall what I tried to say in my Second Lecture about the context theorem of meaning; about meaning as the delegated efficacy of signs by which they bring together into new unities the abstracts, or aspects, which are the missing parts of their various contexts, you will recollect some insistence that a word is normally a substitute for (or means) not one discrete past impression but a combination of general aspects. Now that is itself a summary account of the principle of metaphor. In the simplest formulation, when we use a metaphor we have two thoughts of different things active together and supported by a single word, or phrase, whose meaning is a resultant of their interaction.

"As to metaphorical expression," said Dr. Johnson, "that is a great excellence in style, when it is used with propriety, for it gives you two ideas for one." He is keeping, you see, to the limited traditional view of metaphor. As to the excellence of a style that gives you two ideas for one, that depends on what the two ideas do to one another, or conjointly do for us. We find, of course, when we look closer that there is an immense variety in these modes of interaction between co-present thoughts, as I will call them, or, in terms of the context theorem, between different missing parts or aspects of the different contexts of a word's meaning. In practice, we distinguish with marvellous skill between these modes of interaction, though our skill varies. The Elizabethans, for example, were far more widely skilled in the use of metaphor — both in utterance and in interpretation — than we are. A fact which made Shakespeare possible. The 18th Century narrowed its skill down, defensively, to certain modes only. The early 19th Century revolted against this and specialized in other modes. The later 19th Century and my generation have been recovering from these two specializations. That, I suggest, is a way of reformulating the Classic-Romantic antithesis which it would be interesting to try out.

But it could not be tried out without a better developed theory of metaphor than is yet available. The traditional theory noticed only a few of the modes of metaphor; and limited its application of the term *metaphor* to a few of them only. And thereby it made metaphor seem to be a verbal matter, a shifting and displacement of words, whereas fundamentally it is a borrowing between and intercourse of *thoughts,* a transaction between contexts. *Thought* is metaphoric, and proceeds by comparison, and the metaphors of language derive therefrom. To improve the theory of metaphor we must remember this. And the method is to take more note of the skill in thought which we possess and are intermittently aware of already. We must translate more of our skill into discussable science. Reflect better upon what we do already so cleverly.

Raise our implicit recognitions into explicit distinctions.

As we do so we find that all the questions that matter in literary history and criticism take on a new interest and a wider relevance to human needs. In asking how language works we ask about how thought and feeling and all the other modes of the mind's activity proceed, about how we are to learn to live and how that "greatest thing of all," a command of metaphor — which is great only because it is a command of life — may best, in spite of Aristotle, "be imparted to another." But to profit we must remember, with Hobbes, that "the scope of all speculation is the performance of some action or thing to be done" and, with Kant, that — "We can by no means require of the pure practical reason to be subordinated to the speculative, and thus to reverse the order, since every interest is at last practical, and even that of the speculative reason is but conditional, and is complete only in its practical use." Our theory, as it has its roots in practice, must also have its fruit in improved skill. "I am the child," says the Sufi mystic, "whose father is his son, and the wine whose vine is its jar," summing up so the whole process of that meditation which does not forget what it is really about.

This much has been an introduction or preparation to put the theory of metaphor in a more important place than it has enjoyed in traditional Rhetoric. It is time to come down from these high speculations to consider some simple steps in analysis which may make the translation of our skill with metaphor into explicit science easier. A first step is to introduce two technical terms to assist us in distinguishing from one another what Dr. Johnson called the two ideas that any metaphor, at its simplest, gives us. Let me call them the tenor and the vehicle. One of the oddest of the many odd things about the whole topic is that we have no agreed distinguishing terms for these two halves of a metaphor—in spite of the immense convenience, almost the necessity, of such terms if we are to make any analyses without confusion. For the whole task is to compare the different relations which, in different cases, these two members of a metaphor hold to one another, and we are confused at the start if we do not know which of the two we are talking about. At present we have only some clumsy descriptive phrases with which to separate them. 'The original idea' and 'the borrowed one'; 'what is really being said or thought of' and 'what it is compared to'; 'the underlying idea' and 'the imagined nature'; 'the principal subject' and 'what it resembles' or, still more confusing, simply 'the meaning' and 'the metaphor' or 'the idea' and 'its image.'

How confusing these must be is easily seen, and experience with the analysis of metaphors fully confirms the worst expectations. We need the word 'metaphor' for the whole double unit, and to use it sometimes for one of the two components in separation from the other is as injudicious as that other trick by which we use 'the meaning' here sometimes for the work that the whole double unit does and sometimes for the other component — the tenor, as I am calling it — the underlying idea or principal subject which the vehicle or figure means. It is not surprising that the detailed analysis of metaphors, if we attempt it with such slippery terms as these, sometimes feels like extracting cube-roots in the head. Or, to make a more exact comparison, what would the most elementary arithmetic feel like, if we used the word *twelve* (12) sometimes for the number one (1), sometimes for the number two (2) and sometimes for the number twenty-one (21) as well, and had somehow to remember, or see, unassisted by our notation, which uses we were making of it at different places in our calculations? All these words, *meaning, expression, metaphor, comparison, subject, figure, image,* behave so, and when we recognize this we need look no further for a part, at least, of the explanation of the backward state of the study. Why rhetoricians have not long ago remedied this defect of language for their purpose, would perhaps be a profitable matter for reflection. I do not know a satisfactory answer. As the best teacher I ever knew, G. E. Moore, once remarked, "Why we should use the same form of verbal expression to convey such different meanings is more than I can say. It seems to me very curious that language should have grown up as if it were expressly designed to mislead philosophers; and I do not know why it should have."

The words 'figure' and 'image' are especially and additionally misleading here. They both sometimes stand for the whole double unit and sometimes for one member of it, the vehicle, as opposed to the other. But in addition they bring in a confusion with the sense in which an image is a copy or revival of a sense-perception of some sort, and so have made rhetoricians think that a figure of speech, an image, or imaginative comparison, must have something to do with the presence of images, in this other sense, in the mind's eye or the mind's ear. But, of course, it need not. No images of this sort need come in at any point. We had one instance of the vicious influence of this red-herring in my first lecture — Lord Kames' antic with the mental picture he supposed we must form of Shakespeare's peacock-feather. Whole schools of rhetoric and criticism have gone astray after it. Lessing's discussion of the relations of the arts, for example, is grievously spoilt by it. We cannot too firmly recognize that how a figure of speech works has nothing necessarily to do with how any images, as copies or duplicates of sense perceptions, may, for reader or writer, be backing up his words. In special cases for certain readers they may come in — then is a long chapter of individual psychology which is relevant here. But the words can do almost anything without them, and we must put no assumption about their necessary presence into our general theory.

I can illustrate both the convenience of such

technical terms as *tenor* and *vehicle* and the evil influence of the imagery assumption, with another citation from Lord Kames, from Chapter 20, paragraph 6, of his *Elements of Criticism.* You will see from the very difficulty of making out just what he is saying, how much we need rigid technicalities here. His point is, I think, evidently mistaken; but before we can be satisfied that it is mistaken, we have to be certain what it is; and what I want first to direct your attention upon is the clumsy and distracting language in which he has to state it. He is preparing to set up a rule to be observed by writers in 'constructing a metaphor.' He says, "In the fourth place, the comparison . . . being in a metaphor sunk by imagining the principal subject to be that very thing which it only resembles; an opportunity is furnished to describe it (i.e., the principal subject) in terms taken strictly or literally with respect to its imagined nature."

To use my proposed terms — we can describe or qualify the tenor by describing the vehicle. He goes on, "This suggests another rule: That in constructing a metaphor, the writer ought to make use of such words only as are applicable literally to the imagined nature of his subject." That is, he must not use any further metaphor in describing the vehicle. "Figurative words," he says, "ought carefully to be avoided; for such complicated figures, instead of setting the principal subject in a strong light, involve it in a cloud; and it is well if the reader, without rejecting by the lump, endeavour patiently to gather the plain meaning, regardless of the figures."

Let me invite you to consider what is being done here very carefully, for it illustrates, I believe, most of the things which have made the traditional studies of metaphor not very profitable. And notice first how it shows the 18th Century assumptions that figures are a mere embellishment or added beauty and that the plain meaning, the tenor, is what alone really matters and is something that, 'regardless of the figures,' might be gathered by the patient reader.

A modern theory would object, first, that in many of the most important uses of metaphor, the co-presence of the vehicle and tenor results in a meaning (to be clearly distinguished from the tenor) which is not attainable without their interaction. That the vehicle is not normally a mere embellishment of a tenor which is otherwise unchanged by it but that vehicle and tenor in co-operation give a meaning of more varied powers than can be ascribed to either. And a modern theory would go on to point out that with different metaphors the relative importance of the contributions of vehicle and tenor to this resultant meaning varies immensely. At one extreme the vehicle may become almost a mere decoration or coloring of the tenor, at the other extreme, the tenor may become almost a mere excuse for the introduction of the vehicle, and so no longer be 'the principal subject.' And the degree to which the tenor is imagined "to be that very thing which it only resembles" also varies immensely.

These are differences I return to next week. Let us study Lord Kames a little longer first: How about this suggested rule that we should carefully avoid mounting metaphor upon metaphor? What would be the effect of taking it seriously? It would, if we accepted and observed it, make havoc of most writing and speech. It is disregarding — under cover of the convenient excuse that they are dead — the most regular sustaining metaphors of all speech. It would make, I think, Shakespeare the faultiest writer who ever held a pen; and it turns an obstinately blind eye upon one of the most obvious features of current practice in every minute of our speech. Look, for example, at Lord Kames' own sentence. "Such complicated figures, instead of setting the principal subject in a strong light, involve it in a cloud." What about that 'strong' light? The light is a vehicle and is described — without anyone experiencing the least difficulty — by a secondary metaphor, a figurative word. But you may say, "No! *Strong* is no longer a figurative word as applied to light. It is as literally descriptive of light as it is of a man or a horse. It carries not two ideas but one only. It has become 'adequated,' or is dead, and is no longer a metaphor." But however stone dead such metaphors seem, we can easily wake them up, and, if Kames were right,

to wake them up would be to risk involving the
tenor in a cloud, and nothing of the sort happens.
This favourite old distinction between dead and living metaphors (itself a two-fold metaphor) is, indeed, a device which is very often a hindrance to
the play of sagacity and discernment throughout the
subject. For serious purposes it needs a drastic
re-examination.

We are in fact immeasurably more adroit in han-
dling complicated metaphors than Kames will allow
us to be. He gives an example of a breach of his
rule which is worth examining if only to show how
easily a theory can paralyse normal aptitude in such
things. He takes these two lines

> A stubborn and unconquerable flame
> Creeps in his veins and drinks the streams of life.

"Let us analyse this expression," he says. "That
a fever may be imagined a flame, I admit; though
more than one step is necessary to come at the resemblance." I, for my part, would have supposed,
on the contrary, that we could hardly find a simpler
transference, since both a fever and a flame are instances of a rise in temperature! But he goes on
to detail these steps. "A fever by heating the body,
resembles fire; and it is no stretch to imagine a
fever to be a fire. Again, by a figure of speech,
flame may be put for fire, because they are commonly conjoined; and therefore a fever may be
termed a flame. But now, admitting a fever to be
a flame, its effects ought to be explained in words

that agree literally to a flame. This rule is not observed here ; for a flame drinks figuratively only, not properly."

Well and good ! But who, for all that, has any difficulty in understanding the lines? The interactions of tenor and vehicle are not in the least hampered by the secondary vehicle.

I have taken this instance of vain pedantry chiefly to accustom you to my use of these technical terms, but partly too to support the contention that the best part of the traditional discussion of metaphor is hardly more than a set of cautionary hints to over-enthusiastic schoolboys, hints masquerading as fundamental theory of language. Lord Kames is not exceptionally limited in his treatment or abnormally obtuse. You will find similar things in Johnson when he discusses Cowley and Donne for example, in Monboddoe, and Harris and Withers, and Campbell, in all the chief 18th Century Rhetoricians.

Not until Coleridge do we get any adequate setting of these chief problems of language. But Coleridge's thought has not even yet come into its own. And, after Coleridge, in spite of the possibilities which he opened, there was a regrettable slackening of interest in the questions. The 18th Century was mistaken in the way it put them and in the technique it attempted to use, but it at least knew that they were important questions and that there is unlimited work to be done upon them. And so Lord Kames' *Elements of Criticism*, though I may seem to have been making fun of it in places, and though it is so full of similar things as to be most absorbing reading, is still a very valuable and instructive book offering a model not only of misconceptions to be avoided but of problems to be taken up, reframed and carried forward. Turning his pages you will again and again find points raised, which, if his treatment of them is unsatisfactory, are none the less points that no serious study of language should neglect. One such will serve me as a peg for a pair of warnings or morals of which any ambitious attempt to analyse metaphors is constantly in need.

Kames quotes from *Othello* the single line

Steep'd me in poverty to the very lips

and comments, "The resemblance is too faint to be agreeable — Poverty must here be conceived to be a fluid which it resembles not in any manner." Let us look at Othello's whole speech. We shall find that it is not an easy matter to explain or justify that 'steep'd.' It comes, you will recall, when Othello first openly charges Desdemona with unfaithfulness,

>   Had it pleas'd heaven
> To try me with affliction, had he rain'd
> All kinds of sores, and shames, on my bare head,
> Steep'd me in poverty to the very lips,
> Given to captivity me and my utmost hopes,
> I should have found in some part of my soul
> A drop of patience; but alas! to make me
> The fixed figure for the time of scorn
> To point his slow and moving finger at;

Yet could I bear that too ; well, very well.
But there, where I have garner'd up my heart,
Where either I must live or bear no life,
The fountain from the which my current runs,
Or else dries up ; to be discarded thence !
Or keep it as a cistern for foul toads
To knot and gender in !

What are we to say of that word *steep,* how answer
Kames?   He is indeed too mild, in saying "the resemblance is too faint to be agreeable."   It's not a
case of a lack of resemblance but of too much di-
versity, too much sheer oppositeness.   For Poverty,
the tenor, is a state of deprivation, of desiccation ;
but the vehicle — the sea or vat in which Othello is
to be steeped — gives an instance of superfluity.   In
poverty all is outgoing, without income ; were we
"steeped to the very lips" it would be the incomings
that we would have to fight against.*   You will have
noticed that the whole speech returns again and
again to these liquid images : "had they rained," "a
drop of patience," "The fountain from the which
my current runs, Or else dries up."   None of these
helps *steep* out, and one of them "a drop of patience"
makes the confused, disordered effect of *steep* seem
much worse.   I do not myself find any defence of
the word except this, which seems indeed quite sufficient — as dramatic necessities commonly are — that
Othello is himself horribly disordered, that the utterance is part of "the storm of horrour and outrage"

* In the partly parallel 'And steep my senses in forgetfulness' (*Henry
IV*, P. II, III, i) Lethe, by complicating the metaphor, removes the
difficulty.

with which he is assailing Desdemona and that a momentarily deranged mind speaks so and *is* obsessed with images regardless of their fittingness. Othello, we might say, is drowning in this storm, (Cf. Act II, i, 212-21) and knows it.

The morals I would point with this instance are : First, that not to see how a word *can* work is never by itself sufficient proof that it will not work. Second, conversely, that to see how it ought to work will not prove that it does. Any detailed examination of metaphor brings us into such risk of pedantry and self-persuasion, that these morals seem worth stress. Yet a critical examination of metaphor, with these morals in mind, is just now what literary criticism chiefly needs.

To come back to Kames, his objection that "the resemblance is too faint to be agreeable" (notice the amusing assumption that a writer must of course always aim to be agreeable !) — assumed that tenor and vehicle must be linked by their resemblance and that their interaction comes about through their resemblance one to another. And yet Kames himself elsewhere takes some pride, and justifiably, in pointing out a type of figure which does not depend upon resemblance but upon other relations between tenor and vehicle. He says that it has been overlooked by former writers, and that it must be distinguished from other figures as depending on a different principle.

"*Giddy brink, jovial wine, daring wound* are examples of this figure. Here are adjectives that can-

not be made to signify any quality of the substan-
tives to which they are joined : a *brink,* for example,
cannot be termed *giddy* in a sense, either proper or
figurative, that can signify any of its qualities or
attributes. When we examine attentively the expression, we discover that a *brink* is termed *giddy*
from producing that effect in those who stand on
it. . . How," he asks, "are we to account for this
figure, which we see lies in the thought (I am not
sure what *lies* means here. I think he means 'has
its ground or explanation in the thought' not 'utters
falsehood.') and to what principle shall we refer it?
Have the poets a privilege to alter the nature of
things, and at pleasure to bestow attributes upon a
subject to which they do not belong?" Most moderns would say "Of course, they have !" But Kames
does not take that way out. He appeals instead to a
principle of contiguous association. "We have had
often occasion to inculcate, that the mind passeth easily and sweetly along a train of connected objects, and,
when the objects are intimately connected, that it is
disposed to carry along the good or bad properties of
one to another, especially when it is in any degree in-
flamed with these properties." He then lists eight va-
rieties of these contiguous inflammations — without, I
think, at all clearly realizing what an immense extension of the theory of possibilities of metaphoric interaction he has made with this new principle. Once
we begin 'to examine attentively' interactions which
do not work through *resemblances* between tenor and
vehicle, but depend upon other relations between

them including *disparities,* some of our most prevalent, over-simple, ruling assumptions about metaphors as comparisons are soon exposed.

But let us take one more glance at this *giddy
brink* first.   Is Kames right in saying that a *brink*
cannot be termed *giddy* in a sense that can signify
any of its qualities or attributes?   Is he right in
turning *giddy* into *giddy-making* — "a brink is
termed giddy from producing that effect in those
who stand on it"?   Is it not the case that at the moment of giddiness the brink itself is perceived as
swimming?   As the man totters in vertigo, the
world spins too and the brink becomes not merely
giddy-making but actually vertiginous, seems itself
to stagger with a dizziness and to whirl with a be-
wildering rapidity.   The eyes nystagmically rolling
give away their motion to the world — including the
brink.   Thus the brink as perceived, which is the
brink that the poet is speaking of, actually itself ac-
quires a giddiness.   If so, we may doubt for a moment whether there is a metaphor here at all — until
we notice how this whirling that infects the world
as we grow giddy comes to it by a process which is
itself radically metaphoric.   Our eyes twitch, but
it is the world which seems to spin.   So it is with a
large part, perhaps, in the final account, with *all* our
perceptions.   Our world is a projected world, shot
through with characters lent to it from our own life.
"We receive but what we give."   The processes of
metaphor in language, the exchanges between the

meanings of words which we study in explicit verbal metaphors, are super-imposed upon a perceived world which is itself a product of earlier or unwitting metaphor, and we shall not deal with them justly if we forget that this is so. That is why, if we are to take the theory of metaphor further than the 18th Century took it, we must have some general theorem of meaning. And since it was Coleridge who saw most deeply and clearly into this necessity, and, with his theory of the imagination, has done most to supply it, I may fittingly close this Lecture with a passage from Appendix C of *The Statesman's Manual,* in which Coleridge is stating that theory symbolically.

A symbol, for him, is a translucent instance, which "while it enunciates the whole, abides itself as a living part of that unity of which it is the representative." So here he takes the vegetable kingdom, or any plant, as an object of meditation through and in which to see the universal mode of imagination — of those metaphoric exchanges by which the individual life and its world grow together. If we can follow the meditation we are led, I believe, to Coleridge's conception of imaginative growth more easily and safely than by any other road. For, as the plant here is a symbol, in his sense, of all growth, so the passage too is itself a symbol, a translucent instance, of imagination.

He has been speaking of the book of Nature that "has been the music of gentle and pious minds in all ages, it is the poetry of all human nature, to read it likewise in a figurative sense, and to find therein correspondences and symbols of the spiritual world.

"I have at this moment before me, in the flowery meadow, on which my eye is now reposing, one of its most soothing chapters, in which there is no lamenting word, no one character of guilt or anguish. For never can I look and meditate on the vegetable creation, without a feeling similar to that with which we gaze at a beautiful infant that has fed itself asleep at its mother's bosom, and smiles in its strange dream of obscure yet happy sensations. The same tender and genial pleasure takes possession of me, and this pleasure is checked and drawn inward by the like aching melancholy, by the same whispered remonstrance, and made restless by a similar impulse of aspiration. It seems as if the soul said to herself : From this state hast *thou* fallen ! Such shouldst thou still become, thy Self all permeable to a holier power ! thy self at once hidden and glorified by its own transparency, as the accidental and dividuous in this quiet and harmonious object is subjected to the life and light of nature which shines in it, even as the transmitted power, love and wisdom, of God over all, fills and shines through nature ! But what the plant is, by an act not its own and unconsciously — that must thou make thyself to become ! must by prayer and by a watchful and unresisting spirit, join at least with the preventive and assisting grace to make thyself, in that light of conscience which inflameth not, and with that knowledge which puffeth not up !

"But further. . . I seem to myself to behold in the quiet objects on which I am gazing, more than an arbitrary illustration, more than a mere simile, the work of my own fancy. I feel an awe, as if there were before my eyes the same power as that of the reason — the same power in a lower dignity, and therefore a symbol established in the truth of things. I feel it alike, whether I contemplate a single tree or flower, or meditate on vegetation throughout the world, as one of the great organs of the life of nature. Lo ! — with the rising sun it commences its outward life and enters into open communion with all the elements at once assimilating them to itself and to each other. At the same moment it strikes its roots and unfolds its leaves, absorbs and respires, steams forth its cooling vapour and finer fragrance, and breathes a repairing spirit, at once the food and tone of the atmosphere, into the atmosphere that feeds *it*. Lo ! — at the touch of light how it returns an air akin to light, and yet with the same pulse effectuates its own secret growth, still contracting to fix what expanding it had refined. Lo ! — how upholding the ceaseless plastic motion of the parts in the profoundest rest of the whole, it becomes the visible *organismus* of the whole silent or elementary life of nature and therefore, in incorporating the one extreme becomes the symbol of the other ; the natural symbol of that higher life of reason."

What Coleridge has here said of this "open communion" is true also of the word — in the free metaphoric discursive sentence. "Are not words," he
had asked nineteen years before, "Are not words
parts and germinations of the plant?"

LECTURE VI

METAPHOR (continued)

All life therefore comes back to the question of our speech, the medium through which we communicate with each other ; for all life comes back to the question of our relations with one another.— Henry James, *The Question of our Speech.*

LECTURE VI

THE COMMAND OF METAPHOR

WHEN, in my last lecture, I spent so much time upon Lord Kames' theories of metaphor it was because he, better than anyone else I know, illustrates the limitations of traditional treatment, and shows why these limitations are unnecessary. The neglect of the study of the modes of metaphor in the later 19th Century was due, I think, to a general feeling that those methods of inquiry were unprofitable, and the time was not ripe for a new attack. I am not sure that it is yet ripe in spite of all that Coleridge and Bentham did towards ripening it. Very likely a new attempt must again lead into artificialities and arbitrarinesses. If so, their detection may again be a step on the road. In this subject it is better to make a mistake that can be exposed than to do nothing, better to have any account of how metaphor works (or thought goes on) than to have none. Provided always that we do not suppose that our account really tells us what happens — provided, that is, we do not mistake our theories for our skill, or our descriptive apparatus for what it describes. That is the recurrent mistake which the 18th Century doctrines exemplify and that all doctrines are likely to exemplify unless we are on our guard against it. It is what William

James called the Psychologist's Fallacy, the mistaking of a doctrine, which may be good as far as it
goes, for the very processes it is about.   As if, to use
Bridges' lines from *The Testament of Beauty*,

> as if the embranglements
> of logic wer the prime condition of Being,
> the essence of things ; and man in the toilsome journey
> from conscience of nothing to conscient ignorance
> mistook his tottery crutch for the main organ of life.

Our skill with metaphor, with thought, is one thing
— prodigious and inexplicable ; our reflective awareness of that skill is quite another thing — very in-
complete, distorted, fallacious, over-simplifying.   Its
business is not to replace practice, or to tell us how
to do what we cannot do already ; but to protect our
natural skill from the interferences of unnecessarily
crude views about it ; and, above, all, to assist the
imparting of that skill — that command of metaphor
— from mind to mind.   And progress here, in trans-
lating our skill into observation and theory, comes
chiefly from profiting by our mistakes.

Last time I generalized, or stretched, the sense
of the term metaphor — almost, you may think, to
breaking point.   I used it to cover all cases where
a word, in Johnson's phrase, 'gives us two ideas for
one,' where we compound different uses of the word
into one, and speak of something as though it were
another.   And I took it further still to include, as
metaphoric, those processes in which we perceive
or think of or feel about one thing in terms of
another — as when looking at a building it seems to

have a face and to confront us with a peculiar expression. I want to insist that this sort of thing is normal in full perception and that study of the growth of our perceptions (the animistic world of the child and so on) shows that it must be so.

Let me begin now with the simplest, most familiar case of verbal metaphor—the *leg of a table* for example. We call it dead but it comes to life very readily. Now how does it differ from a plain or literal use of the word, in *the leg of a horse,* say? The obvious difference is that the leg of a table has only some of the characteristics of the leg of the horse. A table does not walk with its legs; they only hold it up and so on. In such a case we call the common characteristics the ground of the metaphor. Here we can easily find the ground, but very often we cannot. A metaphor may work admirably without our being able with any confidence to say how it works or what is the ground of the shift. Consider some of the metaphors of abuse and endearment. If we call some one a pig or a duck, for example, it is little use looking for some actual resemblance to a pig or a duck as the ground. We do not call someone a duck to imply that she has a bill and paddles or is good to eat. The ground of the shift is much more recondite. The *Oxford Dictionary* hints at it by defining a 'duck' in this use as 'a charming or delightful object.' An extremely simplified account of the ground here would make it something like this: that some feeling, of 'tender and amused regard,' say, that it is possible to have towards ducks is being felt towards a person.

A very broad division can thus be made between metaphors which work through some direct resemblance between the two things, the tenor and vehicle, and those which work through some common attitude which we may (often through accidental and extraneous reasons) take up towards them both. The division is not final or irreducible, of course. *That we like them both* is, in one sense, a common property that two things share, though we may, at the same time, be willing to admit that they are utterly different.   When I like tobacco and logic, that is no very obvious character that they have in common.   But this division, though it does not go very deep, may at a certain level help us sometimes to avoid one of the worst snares of the study — the assumption that if we cannot see how a metaphor works, it does not work.

Let us go back to *leg* for a moment.   We notice that even there the boundary between literal and metaphoric uses is not quite fixed or constant.   To what do we apply it literally?   A horse has legs literally, so has a spider, but how about a chimpanzee?   Has it two legs or four?   And how about a star-fish?   Has it arms or legs or neither?   And, when a man has a wooden leg, is it a metaphoric or a literal leg?   The answer to this last is that it is both.   It is literal in one set of respects, metaphoric in another.   A word may be *simultaneously* both literal and metaphoric, just as it may simultaneously support many different metaphors, may serve to focus into one meaning many different meanings. This point is of some importance, since so much misinterpretation comes from supposing that if a word works one way it cannot simultaneously work in another and have simultaneously another meaning.

Whether, therefore, a word is being used literally or metaphorically is not always, or indeed as a rule, an easy matter to settle. We may provisionally settle it by deciding whether, in the given instance, the word gives us two ideas or one ; whether, in the terms I suggested last time, it presents both a tenor and a vehicle which co-operate in an inclusive meaning.* If we cannot distinguish tenor from vehicle then we may provisionally take the word to be literal ; if we can distinguish at least two co-operating uses, then we have metaphor.

For example, when Hamlet says :
"What should such fellows as I do crawling between earth and heaven ?" Or when Swift makes the Brobdingnagian King say to Gulliver : "The bulk of your natives appear to me to be the most pernicious race of little odious vermin that nature ever suffered to crawl upon the face of the earth," are *crawling* and *crawl* to be regarded as literal or metaphoric ?

My answer is that they are metaphoric. Hamlet

---

* This carries assumptions about aspect-selection and thing- or idea-making, whose examination would be necessary in a further development.

or man may crawl literally — as babies and big-game hunters undoubtedly do at times — but in both passages there is an unmistakable reference to other things that crawl, to the motions of foul insects, to vermin, and this reference is the vehicle as Hamlet, or man and his ways, are the tenor. By this test, of course, most sentences in free or fluid discourse turn out to be metaphoric. Literal language is rare outside the central parts of the sciences. We think it more frequent than it is through the influence of that form of the usage doctrine which ascribes single fixed meanings to words and that is why I have spent so much time in these lectures inveighing against that doctrine.

Let us consider, now, some of the varying relations between tenor and vehicle. It is convenient to begin with the remark, which you will meet with everywhere, that a metaphor involves a comparison. What is a comparison? It may be several different things : it may be just a putting together of two things to let them work together ; it may be a study of them both to see how they are like and how unlike one another ; or it may be a process of calling attention to their likenesses or a method of drawing attention to certain aspects of the one through the co-presence of the other. As we mean by comparison these different things we get different conceptions of metaphor. If we mean calling attention to likenesses, we get a main 18th Century doctrine of metaphor. Dr. Johnson, for example, praises Denham's lines on the Thames because "the

particulars of resemblance are so perspicaciously collected." These are the lines,

O could I flow like thee, and make thy stream
My great exemplar as it is my theme!
Though deep, yet clear; though gentle, yet not dull;
Strong without rage; without o'erflowing, full.

Here the flow of the poet's mind, we may say, is
the tenor, and the river the vehicle; and it is worth
noting, as an exercise in analysis, that in the last
two lines there is a repeated alternation of the relative positions of tenor and vehicle and of the direc-
tion of the shift between them. "Though deep,
yet clear": the words are literally descriptive of the
vehicle, the river; derivatively or metaphorically
descriptive of the mind. "Though gentle yet not
dull": "gentle" certainly is literally descriptive of
the mind, the tenor, derivatively of the river, the
other way about; but "dull," I suppose, goes from
the river to the mind again. "Strong without rage"
goes, for me, unquestionably from mind to river,
and "without o'erflowing, full" goes back again from
river, does it not? to mind. All through, of course,
it is not etymology but how *we* take the words which
settles these questions.

These details of order are not important to notice in themselves -- though to do so gives practice
in the peculiar sort of attention which is the method
of the whole study. Still, this alternating movement
in the shifts may have not a little to do with the
rather mysterious power of the couplet, the way it
exemplifies what it is describing:

Though deep yet clear ; though gentle, yet not dull ;
Strong without rage ; without o'erflowing, full.

And also it may have something to do with what
Johnson is rightly remarking when he says that "the
flow of the last couplet is so smooth and sweet that
the lines have not been overpraised."

"The particulars of resemblance (between tenor
and vehicle) are so perspicuously collected," that
is a typical 18th Century conception of the kind of
comparison that metaphor should supply, the process of pointing out likenesses — perspicuously collect-
ing particulars of resemblance.   But it does not
really apply as an account of how these lines work.
The more carefully and attentively we go over the
senses and implications of *deep, clear, gentle, strong*
and *full* as they apply to a stream and to a mind, the
less shall we find the resemblances between vehicle
and tenor counting and the more will the vehicle,
the river, come to seem an excuse for saying about
the mind something which could not be said about
the river.   Take *deep*.   Its main implications as regards a river are, 'not easily crossed, dangerous, navi-
gable, and suitable for swimming, perhaps.'   As applied to a mind, it suggests 'mysterious, a lot going
on, rich in knowledge and power, not easily ac-
counted for, acting from serious and important reasons.'   What the lines say of the mind is something
that does not come from the river.   But the river
is not a mere excuse, or a decoration only, a gilding
of the moral pill.   The vehicle is still controlling
the mode in which the tenor forms.   That appears

at once if we try replacing the river with, say, a cup
of tea !

> Though deep, yet clear ; though gentle, yet not dull ;
> Strong without rage ; without o'erflowing, full.

Comparison, as a stressing of likenesses, is not the
whole mode of this metaphor though it commonly
is in 18th Century writing — where, too, the tenor
is usually the most important partner in the metaphor.   The opposed conception of comparison — as
a mere putting together of two things to see what
will happen — is a contemporary fashionable aber-
ration, which takes an extreme case as the norm.
Here it is, in a summary and exaggerated form.
This is André Breton, the leader of the French
Super-Realists, stating the doctrine very plainly :
    "To compare two objects, as remote from one
another in character as possible, or by any other
method put them together in a sudden and striking
fashion, this remains the highest task to which poetry
can aspire."   (*Les vases communicants.*)
    " 'To put them together in a sudden and striking
fashion' "—"*les mettre en presence d'une manière
brusque et saisissante.*"   That, as "the highest task
to which poetry can aspire" !   It is a doctrine well
worth some examination.   Like Mr. Max Eastman,
with his insistence (in *The Literary Mind*) that
metaphor works by attempting 'impracticable iden-
tifications,' M. Breton sees no need to consider what
should be put with what — provided they are sufficiently remote from one another — nor does he

distinguish between the very different effects of such collocations.   This is the opposite position from Johnson's, for whereas Johnson objected to comparisons being, like Cowley's, 'far fetched,' it is the distance of the fetching here which is the merit.   Mr. Eastman shares this indifference as to the precise effect of the encounter of disparates.   For him the poet "communicates a kind of experience not elsewhere accessible" and, to do so, Mr. Eastman says, he "must arouse a reaction and yet impede it, creating a tension in our nervous system sufficient and rightly calculated to make us completely aware that we are living something — and no matter what." (*The Literary Mind,* p. 205.)   "No matter what?" These last words are heroic certainly.   Tie a man down and approach him with a red-hot poker ; you will arouse a reaction and sufficiently impede it to make him completely aware, I believe, that he is living something.   This same heroism haunts a good deal of current literary theory and practice — not only in the Super-Realists' cult of artificial paranoias.   It comes, I think, from a crude conception of the mode of action of metaphors, a conception which is an excessive reaction from the sort of thing we had last week in Lord Kames.

Let us consider more closely what happens in the mind when we put together — in a sudden and striking fashion — two things belonging to very different orders of experience.   The most important happenings — in addition to a general confused reverberation and strain — are the mind's efforts to connect

THE COMMAND OF METAPHOR

them. The mind is a connecting organ, it works
only by connecting and it can connect any two
things in an indefinitely large number of different
ways. Which of these it chooses is settled by reference to some larger whole or aim, and, though we
may not discover its aim, the mind is never aimless.
In all interpretation we are filling in connections,
and for poetry, of course, our freedom to fill in —
the absence of explicitly stated intermediate steps —
is a main source of its powers.   As Mr. Empson well
says (in his *Seven Types of Ambiguity,* p. 32),
"Statements are made as if they were connected,
and the reader is forced to consider their relations
for himself. The reason why these statements
should have been selected is left for him to invent ;
he will invent a variety of reasons and order them
in his own mind. This is the essential fact about
the poetical use of language."   The reader, I would
say, will try out various connections, and this experi-
mentation — with the simplest and the most complex, the most obvious and the most recondite collocations alike — is the movement which gives its
meaning to all fluid language.

As the two things put together are more remote,
the tension created is, of course, greater.   That tension is the spring of the bow, the source of the
energy of the shot, but we ought not to mistake the
strength of the bow for the excellence of the shoot-
ing ; or the strain for the aim.   And bafflement is an
experience of which we soon tire, and rightly.   But,
as we know, what seems an impossible connection,

UNIVERSITY OF WINCHESTER
LIBRARY

an 'impracticable identification,' can at once turn
into an easy and powerful adjustment if the right
hint comes from the rest of the discourse.   Here
is an instance.

An incautious recent writer on the general theory
of language says: "In England the symbol *house*
may symbolise a reference to many different kinds
of houses; metaphorically its reference may be so
generalised as to refer to many more other things;
but it can hardly ever have the same reference as,
let us say, *bread*."

That sets us a problem; find an occasion in which
bread may be metaphorical for house, or *house* for
bread.   It would not be hard, I think, to find several — but here is a fairly obvious one, from Gerard
Manley Hopkins.   From that rather distressing and
unhappy poem, *The Drummer Boy's Communion*,
when Hopkins is speaking of the wafer as the dwell-
ing of the Divine Presence.   This is the line:

> Low-latched in leaf-light housel his too huge godhead.

There is no strain, surely, in speaking of the bread
here as the little house, housel.

But it is the rest of the poem that makes the connection easy and obvious, which witnesses to a
general truth.   The mind will always try to find connections and will be guided in its search by the rest
of the utterance and its occasion.

I conclude then that these contemporary exploit-
ers of the crude 'clash them together — no matter
what' view of metaphor are beguiling themselves

with by-products of the process of interpretation and neglecting the more important cares of critical theory. But still one point of importance emerges clearly from examining these exaggerations. We must not, with the 18th Century, suppose that the interactions of tenor and vehicle are to be confined to their resemblances. There is disparity action too. When Hamlet uses the word *crawling* its force comes not only from whatever resemblances to vermin it brings in but at least equally from the differences that resist and control the influences of their resemblances. The implication there is that man should not so crawl. Thus, talk about the identification or fusion that a metaphor effects is nearly always misleading and pernicious. In general. there are very few metaphors in which disparities between tenor and vehicle are not as much operative as the similarities. Some similarity will commonly be the ostensive ground of the shift, but the peculiar modification of the tenor which the vehicle brings about is even more the work of their unlikenesses than of their likenesses.

This has, I believe, very important consequences for literary practice and theory at innumerable points. Insufficient analysis here has led not only to false doctrine and crude reading but to attempts in writing to make words behave in fashions which conflict with the nature of language as a medium. To take the danger of false doctrine first. One of the most influential of modern critics has been T. E. Hulme. His death in the War was a very

heavy loss for many reasons — not least, perhaps, because his doctrine of metaphor was left at a half-way
stage from which, I believe, he would certainly have
developed it.   As it stands, in the interpretation in
which it has been vigorously infective for the last
nineteen years — and especially since his papers on
'Modern Art' and on 'Romanticism and Classicism'
were published in 1924 in the volume called *Speculations* — it seems to me most deceiving.

It says (p. 137) "Plain speech is essentially inaccurate.   It is only by new metaphors . . . that it can
be made precise."   This you will see is only Shelley's point again, and we can accept it, with a demurrer as to some of the implications of 'new' here
— a demurrer that Hulme himself hints on an earlier
page when he says, " 'Works of art aren't eggs,' " and
so need not be fresh or new laid.   But he added
various points about the precision that he supposed
metaphor to aim at, and it is these that give occasion
for mistakes.   "The great aim," he says, "is accurate, precise and definite description."   Poetry,
fluid discourse, as opposed to prose, "is not a language of counters, but," he holds, "a visual concrete
one.   It is a compromise for a language of intuition
which would hand over sensations bodily.   It always
endeavours to arrest you, and make you continuously see a physical thing, to prevent you gliding
through an abstract process."

I have three quarrels with this account.   First
with that *always*.   Only remember Shakespeare and
you will not say that the language of poetry *always*

does anything of this sort. My second quarrel is with the words *visual* and *see :* "make you continuously see a physical thing and prevent you gliding through an abstract process." That is patently false.

> If thou didst ever hold me in thy heart
> Absent thee from felicity awhile
> And in this harsh world draw thy breath in pain
> To tell my story.

You need *see* nothing while reading that, and the words certainly do not work by making you see anything. Besides, you already have the actors to look at. My third quarrel is with this fear of the abstract. The language of the greatest poetry is frequently abstract in the extreme and its aim is precisely to send us "gliding through an abstract process."

> This she? No, this is Diomed's Cressida.
> If beauty have a soul, this is not she,
> If souls guide vows, if vows be sanctimony,
> If sanctimony be the gods' delight,
> If there be rule in unity itself,
> This is not she.

We are not asked by Shakespeare here to perceive beauty, but to understand it through a metaphoric argument as the 'rule in unity itself' and to understand its place in the soul's growth.

What can have happened to make so shrewd and acute a writer as Hulme blunder in this gross fashion? I have two explanations, which combine.

The first is that he is tricking himself with the word *see* into supposing that he means it literally when his doctrine would only be sanctioned if he were using it metaphorically.   Obviously if, in an argument, we say "I see your point!" we are using *see* metaphorically.   So when Hulme wrote *see* and *visual* here, the words are to be taken metaphorically too or the doctrine must be condemned at once. What discourse 'always endeavours' to do is to make us apprehend, understand, gain a realizing sense of, take in, whatever it is that is being meant — which is not necessarily any physical thing.   But if we say "a realizing sense," we must remember that this is not any 'sense' necessarily, such as sense-perception gives, but may be a feeling or a thought.   What is essential is that we should really take in and become fully aware of — whatever it is.

This blunder with the word *see* may seem too crude to be likely.   But the patient toil of scores of teachers is going every day, in courses about the appreciation of poetry, into the effort to make children (and adults) visualize where visualization is a mere distraction and of no service.   And little books appear every few months encouraging just this gross misconception of language.   For words cannot, and should not attempt to "hand over sensations bodily"; they have very much more important work to do.   So far from verbal language being a "compromise for a language of intuition"—a thin, but better-than-nothing, substitute for real experience, — language, well used, is a *completion* and does what the intuitions of sensation by themselves cannot do. Words are the meeting points at which regions of experience which can never combine in sensation or intuition, come together. They are the occasion and the means of that growth which is the mind's endless endeavour to order itself. That is why we have language. It is no mere signalling system. It is the instrument of all our distinctively human development, of everything in which we go beyond the other animals.

Thus, to present language as working only through the sensations it reinstates, is to turn the whole process upside down. It overlooks what is important in Mallarmé's *dictum* that the poet does not write with thoughts (or with ideas or sensations or beliefs or desires or feelings, we may add) but with words. "Are not words," so Coleridge asked, "parts and germinations of the plant? And what is the law of their growth? In something of this sort," he wrote, "I would endeavour to destroy the old antithesis of Words and Things: elevating, as it were, Words into Things and living things too." We must do so if we are to study metaphor profitably. Hulme and the school teachers are forgetting everything that matters most about language in treating it as just a stimulus to visualization. They think the image fills in the meaning of the word; it is rather the other way about and it is the word which brings in the meaning which the image and its original perception lack.

That is one part, I think, of the explanation of

these disorders of thought — the mistaking of *see* and *perceive* in the literal sense instead of a wide and open metaphoric sense. But the other part of the explanation goes deeper : it is the mistaking of what I have been calling the tenor-vehicle antithesis for that between the metaphor (the double unit including tenor and vehicle) and its meaning. These two antitheses are easy to confuse, indeed, it is hard to keep them steadily distinct — especially when *metaphor* (and its synonyms), as I illustrated last time, sometimes means 'vehicle,' sometimes means 'vehicle and tenor together.' Nothing but habituation makes this shift manageable and keeps it from deceiving us. I think it deceived Hulme here — and I know it deceives others. When he says, "The great aim is accurate, precise and definite description" we can agree, if that is saying no more than "the words somehow must make us fully and rightly aware of whatever it is, the language must really utter its meaning." That is, the metaphor (the whole thing, tenor and vehicle together) should mean what it should. But Hulme turns his remark into something about a supposedly needful accuracy of correspondence between vehicle and tenor, and so into something which is false. "Plain speech is essentially inaccurate. It is only by . . . metaphors . . . that it can be made precise. When the analogy has not enough connection with the thing described to be quite parallel with it, when it overlays the thing it describes and there is a certain excess" it is inferior. "But where the analogy is every bit of it necessary for accurate description . . . If it is sincere, in the accurate sense, when the whole of the analogy is necessary to get out the exact curve of the feeling or thing you want to express — there you seem to me (he says) to have the highest verse." In part of this, Hulme is thinking of the whole metaphor and its meaning; in other parts he is thinking of the vehicle and tenor. Something which is obvious and true of the whole metaphor and its meaning thus lends an illusory plausibility to a false view of the correspondence of vehicle to tenor. Hulme seems not to be distinguishing these two couples and it is as fatal to confuse them as it would be in chemistry to mistake the order of complexity of a molecule and an electron, or in algebra, to ignore the brackets. His confidence in a truism — that speech should mean what it should mean — makes him (as I read his pages) certain that vehicle must correspond to tenor — the whole of the analogy be necessary to get out the exact curve — and that, in the sense in which I read him, is not a truism, but an easily demonstrable error, a misdescription of all our current practice.

For one thing, there is no whole to any analogy, we use as much of it as we need; and, if we tactlessly take any analogy too far, we break it down. There are no such limits to the relations of tenor and vehicle as this account puts. The result of the doctrine may be seen in those anxious, over-careful attempts to *copy* perceptions and feelings *in words,* to "hand over sensations bodily," of which modern prose at its most distinguished too often consists. Words are not a medium in which to copy life. Their true work is to restore life itself to order.

The error of mistaking the tenor-vehicle relation for the relation between tenor plus vehicle together and what they mean, has consequences which go far beyond what we are apt to regard (on a limited view) as literary matters. They enter into the ways we envisage all our most important problems. For example, into the question of belief. Must we believe what an utterance says if we are to understand it fully? Does the Divine Comedy, or the Bible tell us something which we must accept as true if we are to read it aright? These are questions that we cannot possibly answer satisfactorily unless we are clear as to the ways in which metaphoric utterances may say or tell us something. Mr. Eliot remarks somewhere of the Divine Comedy that the whole poem is one vast metaphor. It is. And, if so, what is it that we might believe in it? Is it the tenor or the vehicle or their joint presentation; or is it 'that tenor and vehicle are thus and thus related there'? Or is the belief required no more than a readiness to feel and will and live, in certain respects, in accordance with the resultant meaning in so far as we apprehend that meaning—or rather in so far as that meaning apprehends, grasps, takes control of, us? We are accustomed to distinguish between taking an utterance literally and taking it metaphorically or anagogically, but, at the simplest, there are at least four possible modes of

interpretation to be considered, not two. And the
kinds of believing that will be appropriate will as
a rule be different. We can extract the tenor and
believe that as a statement; or extract the vehicle;
or, taking tenor and vehicle together, contemplate
for acceptance or rejection some statement about
their relations, or we can accept or refuse the direc-
tion which together they would give to our living.
We need not go to the Alexandrian schools of early
Christian interpretation, or to the similar exegetical
developments of other religions, to find instances
to show how immense the consequences for belief
of these choices may be. The varying possibilities
of understanding of any metaphoric utterance will
show them.

A 'command of metaphor'—a command of the
interpretation of metaphors—can go deeper still
into the control of the world that we make for ourselves to live in. The psycho-analysts have shown
us with their discussions of 'transference'—another
name for metaphor—how constantly modes of re-
garding, of loving, of acting, that have developed
with one set of things or people, are shifted to another. They have shown us chiefly the pathology
of these transferences, cases where the vehicle—the
borrowed attitude, the parental fixation, say—tyran-
nizes over the new situation, the tenor, and behavior
is inappropriate. The victim is unable to see the
new person except in terms of the old passion and
its accidents. He reads the situation only in terms
of the figure, the archetypal image, the vehicle. But

in healthy growth, tenor and vehicle — the new
human relationship and the family constellation —
co-operate freely; and the resultant behavior de-
rives in due measure from both.   Thus in happy
living the same patterns are exemplified and the
same risks of error are avoided as in tactful and
discerning reading.   The general form of the interpretative process is the same, with a small-scale instance — the right understanding of a figure of
speech — or with a large scale instance — the conduct
of a friendship.

But the literary instance is easier to discuss and
more accessible to investigation.   It is an old dream
that in time psychology might be able to tell us so
much about our minds that we would at last become able to discover with some certainty what we
mean by our words and how we mean it.   An opposite or complementary dream is that with enough
improvement in Rhetoric we may in time learn so
much about words that they will tell us how our
minds work.   It seems modest and reasonable to
combine these dreams and hope that a patient per-
sistence with the problems of Rhetoric may, while
exposing the causes and modes of the misinterpretation of words, also throw light upon and suggest a
remedial discipline for deeper and more grievous
disorders; that, as the small and local errors in
our everyday misunderstandings with language are
models in miniature of the greater errors which
disturb the development of our personalities, their
study may also show us more about how these large

scale disasters may be avoided. That at least was
Plato's hope, as it was Spinoza's belief that there is
but one end for the sciences. "Above all things, a
method must be thought out of healing the understanding and purifying it at the beginning, that it
may with the greatest success understand things correctly." These Lectures, which began by claiming
that the study of Rhetoric must, in a certain sense,
be philosophical, may end with a passage, from the
Timaeus, where Plato is speaking of this hope in
myth.

"The circuits of the years, passing before our eyes,
have discovered unto us number and given to us a
notion of time ; and set us seeking to know the nature of the All ; whence we have gotten us Philosophy than which no greater good hath come, nor
ever shall come, as gift from Gods to mortal kind."
That, if we wrest the words, may seem a singularly
bitter charge to bring against the Gods. But Plato
meant otherwise. He goes on, "Concerning Sound
and Hearing let the same thing be said — that they
also have been bestowed by the Gods to the same
end as sight. For to this end hath Speech been or-
dained, and maketh thereto the largest contribution ; and moreover all that part of Music — hath
been given us for the sake of Harmony, and Harmony, having her courses kin unto the revolutions
in our Soul, hath been given by the Muses to be a
helper to the man who, with understanding, shall
use their art, not for the getting of unreasonable
pleasure — which is commonly esteemed the use of

Music but for the ordering of the circuit of our
Soul which hath fallen out of Harmony, and the
bringing thereof into concord with itself. . . Now
unto the Divine Part in us the motions that are kin
are the Thoughts and Circuits of the All. These
must every man follow, that he may regulate the
Revolutions in his Head which were disturbed when
the Soul was born in the Flesh and by thoroughly
learning the Harmonies and Circuits of the All may
make that which understandeth like unto that which
is understood, even as it was in the beginning; and,
having made it like, may attain unto the perfection
of that Best Life which is offered unto men by the
Gods, for the present time and for the time here-
after."

Lightning Source UK Ltd.
Milton Keynes UK
UKOW02f0136080616

275816UK00001B/73/P